Homeschooling For *Eternity*

SKEET SAVAGE

Homeschooling For Eternity

© 2005 Wisdom's Gate. All Rights Reserved.

Address all inquiries and comments to:
Wisdom's Gate
P.O. Box 374
Covert, MI 49043
Phone: 800-343-1943
Website: www.wisdomsgate.com

Library of Congress Cataloging-in-Publication Data
Savage, Skeet (1953-   )
Homeschooling For Eternity
ISBN# 0-9728139-0-X
1. Homeschooling 2. Parenting 3. Religion 4. Christianity 5. Education

All rights reserved. No part of this book may be reproduced, stored in a retrieval system, or transmitted in any form or by any means-electronic, mechanical, photocopy, recording, or otherwise—except for brief quotations for the purpose of review or comment, without the prior written permission of the publisher. God sees you.

Printed in the United States of America
First Formal Edition

To God be the Glory!

Table of Contents

Dedication and Appreciation..5
Preface: by Mercy Hope..6
Introduction: by Israel Wayne..9
Before We Begin..11
1. The Perfect Homeschool Family...14
2. Reasons for Homeschooling...17
3. Education that Produces Godly Character.......................................23
4. Homeschooling Against All Odds..30
5. Homeschooling Amidst Opposition..37
6. Finding and Giving Real Support..41
7. Establishing God's Order For Your Homeschool............................47
8. Finding Hope at the End of Your Rope..54
9. Comfort and Advice for Single Parents..58
10. Homeschooling in Sickness and In Health....................................65
11. Educational Challenges..69
12. Tuning the Strings of Your Child's Character................................76
13. Biblical Discipline..83
14. Knowing Your Child by Heart...88
15. When Rebellion Hits Home..95
16. Parenting With Jesus..102

17. Ways We Make it Hard...106
18. Maximizing Your Efficiency..111
19. Just Say No to Over-Commitment...............................115
20. What About Socialization?...121
21. Homeschooling in the Light..127
22. Separation from the World...134
23. Servanthood: Being Salt and Light.............................139
24. Teaching the Truth..145
25. Hands-On Homeschooling...150
26. Preparing Children to Serve as Unto the Lord............156
27. Walking By Faith...161
28. Training Stewards for the Kingdom............................166
29. Learning to Let Go..172
30. Turn Off the Voices...180
31. Homeschooling: How You Can and Why You Must...184
Conclusion: An Eternal Perspective..................................191

Cover photo and chapter echoes: Jeanene Tiner

© 2005 Wisdom's Gate. All Rights Reserved.

WISDOM'S GATE
P.O. Box 374, Covert, MI 49043
Phone: 800-343-1943
Website: www.wisdomsgate.org

Dedication and Appreciation

To Jesus Christ—

My precious Lord and Savior, Who truly has redeemed my life from the pit of destruction and restored the years that the locust had eaten. I love You.

To all my children—

Being "Mom" to all of you has been the greatest joy in my life. Each one of you is a cherished and unique gift from above—an eternal treasure. Of all mothers to ever walk this earth, I am most blessed! Press on in Jesus, children. Come what may, be steadfast and faithful to the end! *I'll race you Home!* (Hebrews 12) I love you.

To my grandchildren—

Open your hearts to learn the eternal truths your parents have to teach you. Someday, I'll be watching the shores to greet you when you reach the other side of the river. I love you.

To Mom and Dad—

I am so proud of you! Thank you for the love and support you give…and give…and give… I love you.

To my Kingdom Brothers & Sisters—

My adoption into the Family of God, which brought me into eternal fellowship with each of you, is a gift and a treasure beyond measure. May your love for Him and each other increase. I love you.

To the Ryans—

Thank you for being courageous co-laborers with us on this pilgrim journey. May God bless you for your faithful obedience to His Will, His Way, and His Word. I love you.

Preface
by Mercy Hope

We live in a society that has effectively persuaded the majority of parents that forfeiting ones personal comfort and "freedom" for the purpose of training their own children is too great a sacrifice. But as I look back over my life I am ineffably thankful that I had a mom who was willing to literally invest her life in mine. I knew that as her child, *I came first* and that meant a lot.

My mind goes back to one night—one sentence—that forever engraved that fact in my mind. I was eleven years old and it was a perfect December evening. My younger sisters and I had all piled in with Mom onto her king-size waterbed. We all snuggled down under the blankets as Mom read to us from *The Tales of Ranald Bannerman*.

In the middle of the story my older sister came in with a message that someone from Washington D.C. was on the phone wanting to talk to her. Mom looked up and said, "Tell him I'm reading to my girls—I can talk to him tomorrow." I couldn't believe it! I knew Mom was protective of our nightly reading times but this was a little extreme. I mean, the famous gentleman on hold was an IMPORTANT PERSON! That little action engraved in my heart and mind that we were more important to her than *anyone*.

Even though I'm now an adult I still watch Mom's life and learn from her example. For instance, unlike her daughter, Mom thinks very little about where she lands on the public opinion polls. She lives her life almost completely free of the "fear of man." Whether her mailbox is overflowing with fan mail or loaded with criticism for a less than vogue stand she's taken, she remains consistent. She would just as soon sit in her room and talk to her kids as be on National television or speak at a Women's Conference—actually, if you asked her, she would tell you she prefers it.

Growing up, most of the kids my age were afraid of my mom because they only saw the seemingly austere, "Thus saith the Lord" and "No, you can't do such-and-such" side of her. When I would tell her the different comments my friends would make about her being strict, an amused smile would flash across her face and she'd say, "I wish *my* young'uns were a little *more* afraid of me."

Mom was, and is, a woman of high standards, and high expectations for her children. Dating? Don't ask. Youth group? Waste of time. Staying up all night with friends? Can you say "Eleven o'clock sharp"? "Hanging out" was something you did with the laundry and "vegging out" was what we were at the end of gardening season. "Freaking out" was simply not allowed.

I never tried the reasoning tactics that other kids used to manipulate their parents like, "everyone else is doing it." No, that wouldn't have worked with my mom. In fact, it would inescapably have landed me in a lengthy discussion followed by a thesis assignment on, "The Dangers Of Negative Peer Pressure" or, "Why I Need To Be A Leader"—and, at the time, I did *not* enjoy writing.

I have to admit, sometimes Mom's expectations seemed so high that I didn't think I could live up to them, but I kept trying. I know there were times when I wasn't quite turning out like she had hoped, but if she felt like giving up, she never did.

If you know my mom, I think you'll agree with me—Mom is totally unique. I still laugh when I'm on my way out the door to do yard work and hear Mom call after me, "If you chop your legs off with that lawn mower don't come runnin' to me!"

I smile when I think back to when I was a little girl and every once in a while Mom would wake me up just as the sun peeked over the horizon so that just the two of us could go out for breakfast—how I loved that uninterrupted one-on-one time together.

I was reminiscing with one of my sisters the other day about how Mom used to take us to the park before Church, so that we could "get our wiggles out" before having to sit still for so long. Not all parents would take those little extra steps for their children but Mom did.

We also have more than our share of not-so-fond memories like the time Mom and I were held up and robbed in Chicago (neither of us are real street smart). But even then Mom turned it into a "teachable moment" and explained that there are times in life when it's "better to be defrauded." (At least we were still alive!)

Mom demonstrated for me the joy that comes from serving others and putting their needs ahead of your own. If someone was in the hospital Mom was often the first one there with flowers, words of faith and a fervent prayer for healing. Whether it was taking chicken soup to a sick neighbor, cleaning house for an elderly widow, or helping a family move who had to be out of their house by the end of the week, she taught me that "true Christianity happens in work clothes."

We have had our share of tearful late-night discussions, and times when we simply agree to disagree, but one thing I know without a doubt is that she was the mom that I needed and without her guidance I wouldn't be the woman I am today.

Sure, there are things that I'll do different if I have children, but there is a lot I'll do just like Mom. And sure, I have my own trail to blaze, but I'm living a legacy and I have big shoes to fill. I will always be "Skeet Savage's daughter" and that's all right with me.

So, dear parents, if you are willing to lay down your life for your children, and train them in God's ways you are promised in His Word—and I am here to testify—that your children *will* one day "rise up and call you blessed."

The early years: ready for a story...

Introduction
by Israel Wayne

One of the advantages of growing up in a ministry family is that you get to observe many other Christian leaders first-hand. Growing up with a mother who was the editor of a national homeschooling magazine, people tend to assume that your family must be perfect. They think that because you know how to lay out a publication and edit articles that you are somehow, inately, more spiritual than "average" people. Having the opportunity to personally know many Christian leaders, I have come to realize that they are just like everyone else in many ways. They struggle, make mistakes and often miss the mark they are aiming for. It helps to know that you are not alone; that others, even those who are well known, have the same struggles you do.

One of the disadvantages of growing up knowing other Christian leaders is discovering how many of them care more about preserving their pristine *image* than they do for the true spiritual condition of their family. On more than one occassion I remember hearing national Christian homeschooling leaders being applauded from an appreciative audience, only to have that leader's child (one of my peers) turn to me and say, "Yeah, if only these people knew what my parent is really like!" I was always saddened by this.

I always knew that my mother was imperfect. She is the first to admit that. I always knew that our family had a long way to go before we reached sanctified perfection. But one thing that could not be said is that my mother was a hypocrite. She always made it clear that she would abandon the publishing ministry if we couldn't walk the talk. I admire that.

Now that I am a parent myself, and my mother is a grandmother several times over, I look back at the trail my mother blazed in the early days of the modern homeschool movement. She never wanted notoriety or to see her name in lights. She never tried to be a "mover and shaker" in the political world, or in Christian leadership circles. She always reminded us that the Lord's work is the only thing that matters. If our labors become about *us*, we need to shut it down.

I really think if Mom wanted to be remembered for doing one thing well, she would desire the simple title of "mother." I respect her dogged determination to do what she felt God was calling her to do despite who approved, what opposed or how impossible it seemed. If not for her and others of her ilk, there would not be a modern homeschooling movement. Those of us in the younger generation of homeschoolers owe a lot to these pioneers.

As her only son amidst five daughters, I think God sent me into her life to make sure that she didn't skate by on Easy Street when it came to parenting. I was hyperactive, strong-willed, learning challenged, attention deficit, and approached almost everything differently than she would. I don't think she did everything right. I think she made mistakes. But I think she did the most important thing right. She was successful in the only realm that mattered.

She passed on to us a spiritual legacy that will follow us as long as we live. We learned apart from abiding in Christ—as she has done for many years—we could do nothing. We learned that it's all about Jesus, and it's not about us. We learned that to have a close family, you have to work hard at it. We learned that if you sin, you repent and you move forward. We learned that there is a cost to being a disciple of Jesus Christ—you won't be popular and you can't be like the rest of the world. We learned, "Only one life, t'will soon be past, only what's done for Christ will last."

I think the fact that Mom asked me to write her introduction, instead of many other nationally-known leaders, demonstrates that she is more concerned about reality (loving her family) than she is with making people *think* she loves her family. That makes *this book* valid and worth your time to read it.

Before We Begin...

"Help! I'm a homeschooling parent!"

Excuse Me?!? I beg your pardon, but if you're looking for a shoulder to cry on, you've come to the wrong place...

Now, don't get me wrong—lest you think that I'm some heartless, ivory tower-dweller who's just not living in the real world, as a homeschooling parent myself, I really do know just how challenging this business of homeschooling can be (which is why, for over fifteen years now, we've gone the extra mile beyond our own homeschooling efforts, to publish our 96-page quarterly the *Home School Digest*!)

However, it is simply beyond my ability to grasp the mentality of parents who would rather be *anything but* parents! I cannot comprehend why a father, who has been away from his family all day, would rather sit alone in a recliner reading the newspaper, than to share a bedtime story with his little ones gathered appreciatively around him. I absolutely cannot fathom how things could ever have gotten so twisted that mothers would prefer to hold a "paying job" rather than a sweet, cuddly baby!

When I see purported "self-help" books that offer "survival" tactics for young mothers who are "forced" to "put up with" their children until school starts again, or so-called "Christian" romance novels that dangle the enticement of an "escape from the drudgery of every-day life" or advertising that extols the glamour of the fast-paced, care-free (childless), business world of big city life, and bemoans full-time homemaking as an unworthy calling, I must confess to you that I simply cannot relate!

On the contrary, in all my years as a homeschooling parent, I've never once had the experience of seeing that big yellow bus go past the house and wishing my children were on it. Even though we enjoy the fellowship of many friends, I can honestly say that there is no company that I enjoy more than that of my own children. Without exception, at every age, and at every stage, I have loved and enjoyed all my children.

Please don't think for a moment that, as more than one dear friend has often accused me, my children are perfect. (I suspect that the mountains of diapers that piled up at my house smelled just as bad as the ones at yours!) Perhaps, the answer lies with the fact that I am fully aware that they are not perfect, *and I don't expect them to be!* (And, thankfully, most of the time, they extend the same courtesy to me!) I count it a blessed privilege to be their mom, and an honor to have been esteemed worthy of the stewardship of their young lives.

So, by today's standards, does that make me weird, or what? Why do parents seem so obsessed with mimicking the flimsy standards of the world? The substance of our very lives is being eaten away by the modern-day plague of greener grass syndrome.

Any parent who finds themselves constantly "fed up" with their children, dreading each new day as sheer drudgery to be merely endured, feeling angry and resentful about the "sacrifices" they are making in order to fulfill their parental role, or jealous of the "freedom" in which others who have simply bailed out on their parental responsibilities may indulge, needs to take serious inventory. That parent doesn't need self-help books, escape retreats, or extensive counseling—that parent needs an old-fashioned revival born out of genuine repentance!

Practically speaking, we can't receive the tender comfort and loving instruction found in the gentle, open arms of our Heavenly Father when we come kicking and screaming, pouring out an endless stream of complaints, and flailing against His faithful attempts to reach us! In order to obtain any lasting measure of success in this life, we must acquire and maintain a right and Godly perspective of our daily lives as He would have us to live. We need to see things God's way and through His eyes.

Some parents feel inadequate for the task of homeschooling. While I did not pursue formal education beyond the ninth grade, at the same time, if folks can be measured by what they learn from their mistakes, I can truthfully say I've had a top-notch education. (Now, I'm not saying I'm proud of the fact but, frankly, more people would learn from their mistakes if they weren't so busy denying the fact that they've made them.) The point is, you can overcome your past failures or present challenges and *"can do all things through Christ"* because He will give you the strength (Philippians 4:13).

Perhaps the enemy has tricked you into believing that your circumstances are too difficult. Maybe your husband (or wife, or family, or church, or...) doesn't support your desire to homeschool. Maybe you're a single parent. You may have children living in open rebellion. Perhaps, you've left a good paying job and are now struggling to make ends meet on a single income. You may be limited by physical disability, long-term illness, or a difficult pregnancy. Perhaps you're being threatened by local officials regarding your decision to teach your children at home. Believe me, I'm no stranger to problems such as these and am fully aware that they are no laughing matter!

This book has not been written by or about the perfect homeschooling family. Rather, it contains the simple testimony and practical advice of a veteran homeschooling single mother who successfully raised six children as she invested her life in full-time service to the Lord while trusting Him to provide for their needs and hold their family together against enormous odds. It was written for those who would like to homeschool but think they can't, "because..." It was written for those who have homeschooled for several (even many) years, yet have somehow lost their vision and focus—maybe even having become so discouraged that they have completely forgotten why they ever thought they wanted to homeschool their children in the first place!

We chose a 31-chapter devotional format to make it simple to profitably assimilate the contents of this book in manageable segments while taking full advantage of the opportunity to carefully and deeply assess various aspects of their walk with God—and their approach to parenting and homeschooling—in light of pertinent Scriptures.

The fact of the matter is, there is no situation that any one of us are facing, that the grace of our God, as evidenced by the truth of His Word, is not sufficient to cover and redeem. Regardless of the problems you face, that is the uncompromising message of hope that you will find on the pages of this book.

So, if you're looking for a friend who will challenge and encourage you to press toward the mark, and will not allow you to settle for anything less than God's absolute best for your life, you've come to the right place! Hopefully, you can wholeheartedly say along with me ...

Praise God! I'm a homeschooling parent!

The Perfect Homeschool Family

What does the perfect homeschool family look like?

We all have a picture in our minds of what this family probably looks like so I am sure we will recognize them on sight whenever we come across them. Their above-average children are always super neat, camera-ready clean, impeccably behaved, and ready to smilingly recite thirty-seven phonics rules—or name all the signers of the U.S. Constitution (and their wives!)—at the drop of a textbook. Their orderly house is so picture perfect, it will probably be featured in the next issue of Better Houses and Homesteads and—at least in *my* mental picture—their refrigerator is always clean!

However, after many years of publishing the *Home School Digest*, we've yet to find this elusive family to grace one of our covers. No, we couldn't even find this family by looking under our own roof!

At the opposite end of the spectrum are those who hopelessly throw up their hands claiming, "Nobody's perfect!" and never even try to reach loftier, nobler goals.

I am always amazed when parents say to me, "You could not possibly understand what it's like to live with a hyperactive child (or a rebellious teenager, or...)—*your* children are *perfect*!" Really? Despite repeated attempts to dispel the myths to the contrary, I often find myself trying to assure other parents that my children (and I!) do live on this side of the Pearly Gates and we know what it's like to war against the world, the flesh, and the devil.

But, for vast numbers of parents, there always seems to be this inevitably frustrating tendency of trying to keep up with the homeschooling Joneses—and, this is where the problems begin. When we look to the world, or our peers or contemporaries, for our standard of measure, we are setting ourselves up for failure.

"For we dare not make ourselves of the number, or compare ourselves with some that commend themselves: but they, measuring themselves by themselves, and comparing themselves among themselves, are not wise" (2 Corinthians 10:12).

When desiring to see how we are measuring up as a family, we should carefully examine ourselves in the only mirror of truth that accurately reflects an untainted, and unpainted, reality. It is God's Word that provides the ultimate and unchanging standard of measure for serious-minded homeschoolers.

Measuring ourselves by "what we used to be" is limited in its effectiveness to enable us to reach perfection. Looking back can tell us how far we've come, but only by setting our sights on the Highest Standard, will we know how far we've yet to go.

"Brethren, I count not myself to have apprehended: but this one thing I do, forgetting those things which are behind, and reaching forth unto those things which are before, I press toward the mark for the prize of the high calling of God in Christ Jesus. Let us therefore, as many as be perfect, be thus minded: and if in any thing ye be otherwise minded, God shall reveal even this unto you" (Philippians 3:13-15).

To reach the perfection that our God intends for us, we must unlearn some habits and attitudes that we've picked up along the way. Those of us who have struggled with a painful past will have to forgive, try to forget, and turn away from those things which only weigh us down and hold us back from ultimate success.

"Wherefore seeing we also are compassed about with so great a cloud of witnesses, let us lay aside every weight, and the sin which doth so easily beset us, and let us run with patience the race that is set before us, looking unto Jesus the Author and Finisher of our faith; Who for the joy that was set before Him endured the cross, despising the shame, and is set down at the right hand of the throne of God. For consider Him that endured such contradiction of sinners against Himself, lest ye be wearied and faint in your minds" (Hebrews 12:1-3).

It is wearying to measure yourself against *anyone* but the LORD, or *anything* but the Word of our God. It is only His Word that perfects us through the power of His Holy Spirit.

"But continue thou in the things which thou hast learned and hast been assured of, knowing of whom thou hast learned them; And that from

a child thou hast known the Holy Scriptures, which are able to make thee wise unto salvation through faith which is in Christ Jesus. All Scripture is given by inspiration of God, and is profitable for doctrine, for reproof, for correction, for instruction in righteousness: That the man of God may be perfect, thoroughly furnished unto all good works" (2 Timothy 3:14-17).

If we had nothing but the Word of our God to teach us, to train us, to guide us, to equip us—it would be enough. I realize this is not a popular opinion. Those who would believe God's Word on this matter will not be popular people. In fact, they may actually be persecuted for such beliefs, but if they bear it patiently, *even that* will make them perfect in God's eyes!

"My brethren, count it all joy when ye fall into divers temptations; Knowing this, that the trying of your faith worketh patience. But let patience have her perfect work, that ye may be perfect and entire, wanting nothing" (James 1:2-4).

Relax! Cease striving. Put away the worldly instruments and standards of measure. Who cares what the relatives are saying? So what if everyone else's teenager is taking (or passed, or failed) the SAT (or any other government standard of measure)? What does it matter if your friend's five-year-old reads at a 7th-grade level and your 9th-grader still has to stop and sound out words?

Just because everyone in the homeschool support group is going to the beach and calling it a "field trip," does that mean your family has to participate? If the government school kids plan a "see-you-at-the-pole" day, do our homeschooled young people really need to mimic the event to prove their spirituality? If you can live up to the standards of the most admired homeschool family you know, will you, then, really be perfect?

It all boils down to this: Who are you trying to please? Whose standards are you striving to attain? As long as you forsake the vain philosophies of this world, base your foundations on the Word of God, and seek to please Him—and Him only—then, in His eyes, *you* will be the perfect homeschool family!

Reasons For Homeschooling

Over the years, I have spoken with thousands of homeschoolers across the country at homeschooling conventions and our Wisdom's Gate Seminars. Whether by phone, letter, or E-mail, I have heard from *Home School Digest* and *An Encouraging Word* readers from as far away as Cairo, Egypt and Katmandu, Nepal. The reasons given for homeschooling are as far-reaching and as varied as the types of people who have chosen this path.

Some are prompted by what I call knee-jerk reactions—the desire to escape what is perceived as a bad local school system, the wish to avoid negative peer influences, the reality of being unable to afford Private or Christian School, and countless other situations. Others are motivated by positive ideology—accelerated or specialized learning opportunities, time together as a family, and a more natural (relaxed) approach to education—inspired by the belief that homeschooling is the best way to train children.

While I will admit that our own initial decision to homeschool would definitely fall into the knee-jerk category, the years have swiftly carried us over to the solid shores of conviction on the matter. Still, we talk to people all over the country who claim, "We tried homeschooling, and it doesn't work."

When pressed as to why they feel homeschooling "doesn't work" the answers usually go something like, "Well, my children weren't really into it," or "I homeschooled them all the way through and they still went out and got into trouble," or, "My husband said he didn't care if I homeschooled the children so I tried homeschooling, but I just got burned out."

Remember the "Try Jesus" campaign? Everything from bumper stickers to lapel pins proclaimed this ingenious approach to bettering one's life! Well, it's back again with a new face—"Try homeschooling." Don't be fooled, my friend. Homeschooling is not something you "try." It is a commitment like marriage—and discipleship. There's no turning back. God intended this method of learning to be a lifelong enterprise.

So much has changed in the last thirty years, and yet, in so many ways, the basic issues are still the same. After all these years of homeschooling, I've noticed that the most common questions people ask regarding homeschooling are still the same now, as when we started, such as, "What about socialization?" One very major change we've seen is that, at this point, almost everybody knows somebody who is homeschooling!

We've seen many of our country's leaders acknowledge (reluctantly, in some cases), and even officially proclaim, homeschooling as legitimate and acceptable. We've heard the testimonies of academic success resulting in student acceptance into the top institutions in our country. We've studied the statistics from several organizations that have conducted surveys that have proven our claims and solidified our beliefs that homeschooling is methodologically superior to the classroom model of education.

On the other hand, we've also seen far too many families "try homeschooling" and fail miserably. We've heard countless excuses as to why some parents "could never homeschool" their children. We've witnessed the anguish of parents who report that although they homeschooled their children through grades K-12, the children grew up and left home (not necessarily in that order) in open rebellion.

Why is this? Doesn't the Bible promise, *"train up a child in the way he should go, and when he is old he will not depart from it"* (Proverbs 22:6)? I've come to realize that the key contingency to this promise does not lie solely in *where* the training takes place but, rather, in the direction (the way) and the purpose (in which he should go) of the training. The scope of the homeschooling lifestyle and the focus of the ultimate goal is, to a large degree, what determines which direction the child will take. If a child seems to be "heading off in the wrong direction," or departing from the way he should go, the responsible parent will diligently examine, in the clear light of God's Word, the breadth and direction of the path on which they have allowed, or even encouraged, the child to walk (Matthew 7:13,14).

There is a vast difference in motivation, approach, and end-results among homeschooling families. There are those who, driven by their overall disdain for authority, and carried away by the spirit of rebellion that so dominates our society, have given full reign to their desire for autonomy by subtly masking their unbridled independence under the guise of homeschooling. These folks have merely taken convenient advantage of the growing cultural acceptance of homeschooling and jumped on the bandwagon of popularity surrounding the contemporary homeschooling movement—for their own selfish purposes.

Others have dutifully noted the homeschooling laws in their state and taken the necessary precautions (whether by actual compliance or through the purchase of what they consider to be the equivalent of "legal insurance"). They've insisted that the government has no business involving itself in the education of children, and then run the gamut of double-mindedness by lobbying for "permission" to homeschool "legally," or demanding that the government fund their children's education through vouchers or cater to their perceived "right" to have their children participate in music, sports and other "benefits" of government programs. They've eagerly grabbed their ever-expanding discount homeschooling catalog and dashed off to the nearest curriculum fair in search of that elusive math/science/phonics program that offers the highest guarantee of mastery with the least amount of effort (and money). They've joined the local support group after carefully studying the "statement of faith" to make sure they won't be forced to experience interaction with anyone who holds a different point of view. They've gone on all the field trips and kept their children immersed in the various social activities of the local culture so that they will easily fit in with their peers in the "real world."

Many fathers avoid involvement as much as possible and magnanimously proclaim, "if Mom wants to homeschool," they "won't interfere." Meanwhile, there are those mothers who hang out on the phone, or cruise the internet looking for chat sessions focusing on the subject of "burnout" while they hold out with white-knuckled anticipation for the monthly "Mom's Night Out."

I realize that we are rocking somebody's boat here, but I've seen far too many families needlessly shipwrecked and desperately flailing around in the perilous waters of adversity, or hopelessly carried off by the swift and deadly current of popular culture, to be afraid of speaking a truth that may offend some while setting others free.

On the other end of the spectrum, there are those who, recognizing their citizenship in a Kingdom that is not of this world, have simply made the commitment to teach and train their own children—

regardless of the cost—out of a heart of obedience born of the conviction that homeschooling is the method mandated by God to be implemented according to God's expressed standard of measure and the Biblical model of discipleship. These faithful families are beginning to reap the blessed fruit of righteousness and holiness as they continue to teach their children, by their own Godly example, to work out their salvation with fear and trembling for the Glory of God (Philippians 2:12).

Ask yourself a few simple questions. Which kind of homeschooler am I? Who am I most afraid of offending—God or the State? By whose standards do I measure myself and my children? In which direction is my homeschooling aimed? Am I moving toward the world, or away from it?

By the grace of God, we must bring homeschooling to its proper place under the Headship and Authority of our Lord Jesus Christ. We must live in complete surrender to His will, and endeavor, in all ways, to obey God rather than men. We must obey His Word, come out from the world and be truly separate—a Holy people set apart for His use, who have consecrated their lives, and their children, for His eternal purpose and Glory.

BEARING PRECIOUS SEED

To give you some perspective on the far-reaching effects of your homeschooling, consider the dandelion. You may not think of a dandelion as "precious seed," but you certainly are aware of the fact that it is "prolific seed"! Like it or not, the persistent dandelion is here to stay!

I, for one, am a dandelion fan! I realize not everyone shares my love for these cheerful little plants. My father, for instance, seems to have a totally different reaction when he sees those bright-yellow gems multiplying all over his carefully-groomed, well-manicured lawn!

My grandmother, on the other hand, recognized the dandelion as the Lord's provision. An invitation to stay for dinner at grandma's house taught me the practical usefulness of these misunderstood weed-flowers. Rather than decoratively gracing the table as a fragrant centerpiece, you'd be more likely to find dandelions served on a plate in the form of greens, or possibly even steeped and enjoyed as a tea. My girls, when they were little, even used the blossoms to color pretty pictures they drew for me and sometimes accidentally—while inhaling the dandelion's unique perfume—colored their noses as well!

Yes, from my earliest childhood, right on through to present-day motherhood, the dandelion has always been a special favorite. Think about it for a moment—what mom hasn't had occasion to rave over the simple beauty of a carefully gathered dandelion bouquet, given with great pride and a heart full of love, by a small child with a beaming face and dirty little hands.

Or, how many of you, while enjoying the serenity of a warm summer evening—or maybe you were relaxing at a picnic on a blanket in the country on a bright, sunshiny day—have found yourself fascinated by the captivating, quintessential beauty of a seeded dandelion? Remember those brief, awe-filled moments when you held one of those incredibly fragile dandelions in your hand and watched those tiny, delicate dandelion seeds drift and float through the air as you gently waved or blew them away? If its been a while since you've indulged yourself with such simple pleasures, you owe it to yourself, and your children, to stop and smell the dandelions!

Though life's travels have taken me many places, my heart is definitely in the country! When business held us in Washington D.C. for a few days, I found myself intrigued by the sights, sounds and happenings of the city. So much to see and do! However, by the dawning of the third day, I experienced a restlessness that I could not explain and found myself searching for a quiet place to collect my thoughts. As I wandered down the concrete sidewalks, along the city streets lined with massive, man-made structures boasting their magnificent architecture, the entire scene struck me as alternately impressive and overwhelmingly oppressive.

I prayed to quiet my soul as I purposefully drew my thoughts away from the things of this world, and turned my eyes toward Heaven, waiting for the Lord to speak to my heart. As I lowered my eyes, there in the crevice, between the walkway and the building, was one, lone dandelion! What a sight for sore eyes! What an energetic burst of vibrant color among so much gray, lifeless matter. The absolute finest that man can conceive and achieve doesn't hold a candle to the splendid beauty and perfection of God's creation. I literally got down on my knees and just marveled at the quiet determination of such a modest and unassuming product of creation!

Later that same day, when the crowds were at their peak, we happened to pass down that same street and I, once again, drew aside—this time to direct my children's attention to this unexpected phenomenon and to ponder with them, for a few moments, the amazing significance of its presence, virtually unnoticed by the hurried masses. Such a seemingly insignificant thing, the humble dandelion has touched all of our lives. For me, it stands as a vibrant and inspiring symbol of determination and perseverance.

Children may grow like weeds, but they must be cared for like tender plants. As surely as there will be dandelions growing next year, the young lives that we, as homeschooling parents, are nurturing today, are going to bear fruit. Whether it be good or bad, our offspring *will* bear fruit. We cannot leave this precious seed to the winds of chance. We cannot wait for ideal conditions, or a more convenient time. We must seize the fleeting moment of their youth to carefully plant, fertilize, water and weed this valuable crop—God's provision for the future.

The product of their adult lives will largely be determined by the seeds we faithfully sow into their fertile young lives today. When that seed comes up, somewhere down the road, it will be obvious to all what our little kernels really contained deep down inside of them. Rooted in the Word of God, lovingly nurtured with tender, devoted care, covered with fervent prayer and steadfast faith, your children can bear a fruit that will be a blessing to all who taste of it, and will bring Glory and Honor to our God.

You don't have to wish on a dandelion for that kind of a harvest. You have His promise—just as sure as His Word—you can count on it! Plant On!

Education That Produces
True Wisdom & Godly Character

When we talk about homeschooling, the concept we set forth could be more specifically defined as Christian character-based education. To understand the distinction between genuine Christian education and that being offered by the government schools, consider the following truths.

ELEMENTS OF GOVERNMENT SCHOOL EDUCATION

Government education typically takes place nine months out of the year although many districts have adopted year-round schooling.

The philosophy of the government school is based on a man-centered accumulation of knowledge without moral application.

The goal or agenda of the government school is to create working-class taxpayers, civic servants, and politically-correct citizens.

The approach or method the government school uses to accomplish this agenda includes an age-segregated classroom context, peer-directed training in subjective values, and rote memorization of disconnected facts.

The motivation given for pursuing education in the government school is self-centered/oriented—engendering self-esteem, self-worth and selfish ambition.

The standard of measure used by the government schools includes tests such as SAT or GED, and college-entrance exams.

The curriculum is selected by the government based on its potential to accomplish their own agenda, while each teacher has his or her own political and moral values to pass along—not to mention the extra-curricular lessons children receive in peer pressure, stereotyping, labeling, and brainwashing with politically-correct propaganda ... and so much more that they have to offer you down there at the government schools!

ELEMENTS OF CHRISTIAN HOMESCHOOLING

In contrast, for the Christian, through the discipleship process, learning is a life experience that never ends.

The Christian philosophy of education is based on an approach to education that brings Glory to God. It is God-inspired, God-motivated, God-driven, God-directed, and God-blessed. *"For in Him we live and move and have our being"* (Acts 17:28).

It is an education directed by God and derived from Him that builds wisdom and understanding (Job 12:13). *"If any of you lack wisdom, let him ask of God, that giveth to all men liberally, and upbraideth not; and it shall be given him"* (James 1:5).

The goal or agenda of Christian character-based education is to develop faithful servants for the Lord (Matthew 25:21) and to produce responsible people with a Heavenly citizenship (John 18:36). In its purest sense, the word *teacher* (educator) means "one who brings out the best in a student" and the Christian parent will seek to do this in such a way that God will receive the glory for it all.

The Christian approach or method for accomplishing this agenda recognizes and employs the intrinsic learning environment of the home as the most natural context for learning through discipleship methodology that is consistent and ongoing. *"And thou shalt teach them diligently unto thy children, and shalt talk of them when thou sittest in thine house, and when thou walkest by the way, and when thou liest down, and when thou risest up. And thou shalt bind them for a sign upon thine hand, and they shall be as frontlets between thine eyes. And thou shalt write them upon the posts of thy house, and on thy gates"* (Deuteronomy 6:7-9).

This type of real learning cannot take place without an acceptance and application of God's Laws. *"But his delight is in the law of the LORD; and in His law doth he meditate day and night"* (Psalm 1:2).

It is an education that is focused not on self, but on others. *"Let nothing be done through strife or vainglory; but in lowliness of mind let each esteem other better than themselves. Look not every man on his own things, but every man also on the things of others"* (Philippians 2:3,4).

The Christian standard of measure is the Bible and nothing but the Bible. *"Study to shew thyself approved unto God, a workman that needeth not to be ashamed, rightly dividing* [correctly handling] *the word of truth."* (2 Timothy 2:15). The wise parent will learn to view homeschooling as a journey recognizing that the Bible is the time-tested map that provides direction along the way.

A truly Biblical approach to learning will guarantee that we do not raise career-driven, workaholics who become overwhelmed with the burdens of this life! Matthew 11: 29, 30 issues a challenge to each one of us, *"Take my yoke upon you, and learn of me; for I am meek and lowly in heart: and ye shall find rest unto your souls. For my yoke is easy, and my burden is light."* When the homeschool load begins to feel *heavy*, you've taken on more than the Lord intended.

Christian homeschooling *is not* a head-in-the-sand approach. It necessitates defining and exposing anti-Christian philosophy and providing a quality of education that will prompt Godly responses to evil influences. The goal is to raise our children to be "wise as serpents and harmless as doves" (Matthew 10:16)—not naive!

OBTAINING TRUE WISDOM

"Where is the wise? Where is the scribe? Where is the disputer of this world? Hath not God made foolish the wisdom of this world" (1 Cor. 1:20)?

Wisdom cannot be obtained independent of God. *"All this have I (Solomon) proved by wisdom: I said, I will be wise; but it was far from me. That which is far off, and exceeding deep, who can find it out? I applied mine heart to know, and to search, and to seek out wisdom, and the reason of things, and to know the wickedness of folly, even of foolishness and madness"* (Ecclesiastes 7:23-25).

True wisdom does not exist apart from God. *"For the wrath of God is revealed from Heaven against all unGodliness and unrighteousness of men, who hold the truth in unrighteousness; Because that which may be known of God is manifest in them; for God hath shewed it unto them. For the invisible things of Him from the creation of the world are clearly seen, being understood by the things that are made, even His eternal power and Godhead; so that they are without excuse: Because that, when they knew God, they glorified Him not as God, neither were thankful; but became vain in their imaginations, and their foolish heart was darkened. Professing themselves to be wise, they became fools"* (Romans 1:18-22).

God's Word is the standard of true wisdom. *"Let no man deceive himself. If any man among you seemeth to be wise in this world, let him become a fool, that he may be wise. For the wisdom of this world is foolishness with God. For it is written, 'He taketh the wise in their own craftiness.' And again, 'The Lord knoweth the thoughts of the wise, that they are vain.' Therefore let no man glory in men"* (1 Corinthians 3:18-21).

God is the ultimate Source of true wisdom. *"If any of you lack wisdom, let him ask of God, that giveth to all men liberally, and upbraideth not; and it shall be given him"* (James 1:5).

God rejects the "wisdom" of this world and its petty religious dogmas. *"Wherefore the Lord said, 'Forasmuch as this people draw near Me with their mouth, and with their lips do honour Me, but have removed their heart far from Me, and their fear toward Me is taught by the precept of men: Therefore, behold, I will proceed to do a marvellous work among this people, even a marvellous work and a wonder: for the wisdom of their wise men shall perish, and the understanding of their prudent men shall be hid'"* (Isaiah 29:13-14).

Godly wisdom is born of the Spirit within us. *"And I* (Paul), *brethren, when I came to you, came not with excellency of speech or of wisdom, declaring unto you the testimony of God. For I determined not to know any thing among you, save Jesus Christ, and Him crucified. And I was with you in weakness, and in fear, and in much trembling. And my speech and my preaching was not with enticing words of man's wisdom, but in demonstration of the Spirit and of power: That your faith should not stand in the wisdom of men, but in the power of God. Howbeit we speak wisdom among them that are perfect: yet not the wisdom of this world, nor of the princes of this world, that come to nought: But we speak the wisdom of God in a mystery, even the hidden wisdom, which God ordained before the world unto our glory: Which none of the princes of this world knew: for had they known it, they would not have crucified the Lord of glory"* (1 Corinthians 2:1-8).

Top honors bestowed on earth are nothing to God. *"Because the foolishness of God is wiser than men; and the weakness of God is stronger than men. For ye see your calling, brethren, how that not many wise men after the flesh, not many mighty, not many noble, are called: But God hath chosen the foolish things of the world to confound the wise; and God hath chosen the weak things of the world to confound the things which are mighty; And base things of the world, and things which are despised, hath God chosen, yea, and things which are not, to bring to nought things that are: That no flesh should glory in His presence. But of Him are ye in Christ Jesus, who of God is made unto us wisdom, and righteousness, and sanctification, and redemption: That, according as it is written, 'He that glorieth, let him glory in the Lord'"* (1 Corinthians 1:25-31).

LEARNING TO SEE AS GOD SEES

"And God saw that the wickedness of man was very great in the earth, and that every imagination of the thoughts of his heart was only evil continually. And it repented the LORD that He had made man on the earth, and it grieved Him in His heart. And the LORD said, 'I will destroy man whom I have created from the face of the earth...for it repenteth me that I have made them'" (Genesis 6: 5-7). *"But as the days of Noah were, so shall it be also in the days of the Son of man"* (Luke 17:25).

These certainly are perilous times. It's hard to imagine Sodom and Gomorrah being more wicked than the world we know today. Sometimes, I just shake my head in wonder that a Holy God can allow such sin to go on and I say, with the Psalmist, "How long, Oh, Lord?"

But, God is not just sitting around with His head in the sand, or idly daydreaming somewhere over the rainbow. Our God *sees*. He *knows*. He is also patient and merciful. (Let's face it, were it not so, you and I would have been fried a long time ago!) With every tick of the clock, He is watching—and waiting.

"For the eyes of the LORD run to and fro throughout the whole earth to shew Himself strong on behalf of them whose heart is perfect towards Him" (2 Chronicles 16:9).

It may seem like just another homeschooling day to you, but you've got a home inspection coming up today. God is checking you out! He's looking for you! Does that make you want to turn on the porch light, throw open the door and wave your hand saying, "Here I am, Lord!" Or, did you just get an incredible urge to run and jump back in bed to hide under the covers?

Whether you realize it or not, you have a test to pass today—and God is looking for a perfect score! What's that you say? Nobody's perfect? Well, consider this—when God went looking for Noah, old Noah passed the test! (With flying colors!) *"But Noah found grace* [favor] *in the eyes of the LORD ... Noah was a just* [righteous] *man and perfect in his generations* [blameless among the people of his time], *and Noah walked with God"* (Genesis 6:8-9).

What a legacy! The amazing thing is that, obviously, God still believes there may be a few Noahs on the earth—otherwise, He would not still be looking! So how do we go about developing that kind of a lifestyle? Where can we find perfection in a sinful world?

The key, as we all know, is to be "in the world, but not of the world." Figuring out exactly how to live in such a way has become the proverbial stumbling block for more than one pilgrim along the way.

We must develop the ability to see the world as God sees it. Shun the rose-colored glasses. Get rid of that high-powered lens that magnifies the imperfections of others and makes things look worse than they really are. Open your eyes and see the world in the true light of day—then, close your eyes and let go of it.

"Love not the world, neither the things that are in the world. If any man loves the world, the love of the Father is not in him. For all that is in the world, the lust of the flesh, and the lust of the eyes, and the pride of life, is not of the Father, but is of the world. And the world passeth away, and the lust thereof, but he that doeth the will of God abideth forever" (1 John 2:15-17).

Everything of earth that makes up our life here is but a vapor (James 4:14) whether it be material possessions (Luke 12:18-20) or physical beauty, or even pain (2 Corinthians 4:16-18). We should hold the things of this world as loosely as we would a red-hot chunk of coal. We should remind our children that it's all going to burn up and be reduced to ash someday (2 Peter 3:10). There is nothing here worth clinging to—and certainly nothing worth missing Heaven for!

The more we come to see ourselves as living in the Kingdom, and not of this world, the more we will find ourselves perfectly in line with God's will and His ultimate plans and purposes for our lives.

So, how about it? Perhaps, down deep in your heart you are longing to be found faithful, and to leave a shining legacy when this life is over, but in the back of your mind, you think that it's an impossible dream. Don't believe it! Have the courage to see yourself as God sees you and forsake every sin that comes to light. Cry out to God with your whole heart and just see how He comes to your rescue! Remember, our God sees. He knows. He hears. *"For the eyes of the Lord are on the righteous and His ears are attentive to their prayer..."* (1 Peter 3:12).

Who are we really wanting to please? God's Honor Roll is determined by a Heavenly standard that defies the "wisdom" of this world. Put aside striving to compete with the world in standardized tests of achievement and begin to focus on higher goals. Get your priorities straight and lined up with God's standard of measure. For the sake of our children—and the lost and dying world around us—we must seek with all our hearts to possess *true wisdom* and Godly character.

Sunday go to meetin' clothes Easter Sunday morning.

Sisters—and best friends!

Getting a little advice from big brother.

Against All Odds: My Own Experience

I am a serious homeschooler. I mean it. I want you to know at the outset—I am 100% sold on homeschooling.

Often, when I am booked as a speaker, folks refer to me as a "veteran" homeschooler. Well, what that means, in a nutshell, is simply this—I was homeschooling when homeschooling wasn't cool!

In the mid '70s when I first began homeschooling my oldest children, the term, "homeschooling" was not even a buzzword. Back then, they just called us, "TRUANT"!

My journey down this road we call homeschooling began when my oldest daughter was two years old. Sony had an insatiable desire to learn and an endless supply of questions. She *had* to know, "Who...?" "What...?" "Where...?" "How...?" "Why...?"—and "Why not?"!

When the time came for Sony to enter Kindergarten, she was excited and ready to go. Even though we were very poor, I was always careful to dress her each day in the best clothes she had and to make certain that they were clean and neatly pressed. We made each day's send-off a big deal, always trying to be bright and positive about the whole experience. I wanted her to be happy and successful in school so that she could avoid the struggles that I had faced.

However, it wasn't long before my joyful, bouncing little daughter became a weepy, clingy child whose daily plea was, "Please don't send me to school. Please let me stay here with you!" She developed hives and constantly complained that her tummy hurt. She no longer slept well through the night and would clam up and fidget every time someone asked, "So, how do you like school?"

Once, when someone asked, "What did you learn in school today, Sony?" she burst into tears. Finally, with gentle but persistent proding, bit by bit, the story began to unfold. It was not a pretty picture that she painted for me.

One day, the teacher had called Sony up to the front of the class where a large wall hanging, depicting the colors of the rainbow, was displayed. Sony was asked to identify the color yellow. Since the colors were shown in various shapes and sizes, she was also asked to distinguish between a circle and a square. While very few of the other students in the class were capable of answering correctly, these were things Sony had known since she was a two-year-old. She felt that she was being mocked and, embarrassed, she began to cry. The teacher responded, "You think you're so smart but you don't even know your colors. Why can't you participate like the rest of the children? You're no better or smarter than anyone else in this class. Go sit down."

Although they were only in school for half a day, the children were all forced to lie down on the floor to take a half-hour nap—something Sony had not needed to do since she was a toddler. When you throw in two recesses and one snack break, there really was not much time for actual teaching or learning. Sony was extremely bored. Even more troubling than this were other problems of a more insidious nature.

During the first few days of school, upon noticing that Sony prayed before eating her sandwich at snack time, the teacher interrupted her prayers one day to explain, "I don't think that is necessary or appropriate here."

The teacher also felt that Sony should try to "fit in" with the other children by dressing as they did and had threatened to not allow her to go out to recess if she did not wear pants to school like the other girls in the class.

Feeling the need to talk with the teacher about these issues, I went to the school an hour before closing. Not wanting to disrupt any teaching that might be going on, I merely opened the door and walked into the classroom and stood quietly. To my utter amazement, I remained there, unnoticed, for a full half hour while the teacher sat over in a corner of the room watching a soap opera—while barking orders over her shoulder for the children to "shut up and sit down!"

When the teacher finally realized my presence, before I could say a word, she flew at me insisting that I had "no right" to come into *her* classroom. When I tried to explain that I had come to discuss my daughter's situation, I was informed in no uncertain terms that

I had no business coming there to check up on her or question her methods. Furthermore, she informed me that she was "well aware" that my daughter had "serious emotional problems and social maladjustments" and that, knowing that she came from a "strict religious home"* the teacher, therefore, had "no trouble figuring out where the problems really lie." (*In truth, we were just your basic carnal, wimpy church-going family at the time—lots of Bible "knowledge," no real relationship with God; and certainly no power to live holy lives according to Titus 1:16.) She proceeded to threaten me insisting that if I ever tried that "stunt" again, she would take strong action. I staggered out of that classroom dazed and appalled.

When Sony returned home that day, I apologized sincerely to her for not really understanding what she had been desperately trying to tell me, and gave her my word that we would come up with some way for her to learn that did not entail sending her to that school. However, since there were no funds for private school, and moving at that point was not an option, that promise seemed easier made than kept.

As I pondered my dilemma, it slowly occurred to me that most of what she already knew I had been able to teach her at home, so I decided that I would just hide out and continue doing that until she reached the age considered appropriate to enter ninth grade—which is about when I figured I would run out of smarts and the children would have caught up with me—if the authorities had not caught up with me first!

So, that is how we began homeschooling.

Over the next summer, I discovered yard sales and began loading up on good books—for both the children and for myself. I also discovered that you could buy educational workbooks, rated all the way through sixth grade, in the toy section beside the coloring books at K-Mart. But, when both of my children had just whipped through these in no time, I knew that I needed to come up with something more challenging.

When a trip to the doctor left me sitting in his waiting room, I saw a magazine ad for a popular correspondence school for grades K-12, and contacted them immediately. However, my hopes were soon dashed as they informed me that they could only sell to me if I resided in another state, or if I were a missionary who wanted to use the material outside of the country. I was advised in no uncertain terms that they could not legally sell curricula to me for my own personal use with my own children in my own home. It just was not done!

Homeschooling book fairs, support groups and state conventions were not in vogue as they are today, nor were homeschooling publications and card packs in abundance. I was afraid to let many people know what I was doing, and I was very careful to keep the children inside and out of sight during "school hours." Still, the school officials were unaccustomed to being confronted with such challenges and were not willing to simply let us slip away quietly.

Every morning that big yellow bus would pull up right outside our door—literally! The road was less than 20 feet from the front door of our tiny little house and that big old school bus absolutely filled the view no matter which of the front windows you looked out. It was an imposing sight to say the least! The bus driver would bellow my name and threaten us with dire consequences "… if those children aren't on this bus when I come back here tomorrow!" Several times, he threw the gears into park and came stomping up on our porch to pound on our door while hollering to get our attention (in case we didn't notice that he was out there, I reckon). Often, he'd sit and blow that horn for up to ten minutes while the neighbors peeked out from behind their curtains. On sunny days, they'd sometimes just march on out in their yards to watch the morning show—always taking time to meet for a few minutes in the drive between their houses to cluck their tongues and shake their heads out of "concern" for their "weird" neighbors.

Then, once the school bus had arrived at its destination—*without* my children—the school principal or the teacher would alternately be on the phone dialing my number. After weeks and months of this kind of harassment, it didn't take caller ID to tell me who was calling me when, without fail, at the same time every day, my phone would begin to ring.

After much wrangling and many threats from the school, that which I greatly feared finally came upon me. An official-looking letter arrived in the mail. I stumbled through the house as I read the ominous words informing me that I must appear at a hearing to defend myself against truancy charges.

In shock, I dropped into the nearest chair, letting the letter fall to the dining room table in front of me, where the children sat doing their "school work." A paralyzing fear overtook me and I lowered my head into my hands in despair. Realizing that my consternation was directly related to the letter, Sony asked if she could read it. I nodded my head affirmatively as my thoughts continued to swirl in dizzying patterns. My brain could hardly believe this was happening. Did that letter say what I thought it said?

Several minutes passed before I reached for the letter again, only to discover that Sony had circled several words with the red pen that I used to make corrections on her school work, and had written the proper spelling alongside the misspelled words, just as I always had her do on her own papers.

Being quite upset already, I wrongly scolded her. "Sony, this is not a school lesson! I need to keep this paper in case we need to refer to it regarding times and dates and such." But, of course, as I paused to study the letter a bit closer and to think about it for a moment, she was right. The words were, indeed, misspelled. As the irony of the situation began to sink in, I apologized for being sharp with her and commended her for her sharp observation. This was a time to pull together—not to fall apart!

With only a week until the hearing, I began to make an appeal to those around me, hoping to gather support for our cause. Thus, it was during this time that I came to understand a universal truth: adversity is life's way of letting you know who your true friends are.

"Friends" at the local church we'd been attending, who had never really said much (to my face) about their views on homeschooling, offered little comfort with remarks such as, "Well, what do you expect? You *are* breaking the law, you know. What makes you think you are any better than anyone else?"

People who had always been quite outspoken about how "bright," "advanced," "charming," and "well-mannered" my children were, quickly back-pedaled when asked for support, explaining that they did "not want to get involved" in our legal struggles.

While I may have had a constitutionally protected "right" to seek and obtain "counsel," actually finding that help in the form of competent legal support was another matter. I spoke with two different lawyers who explained that they could not help me because the law said children have to go to school (which was a lie, but how was I to know?). Besides, when I was informed as to how much that "help" was going to cost me, I realized that, even had I been able to find a lawyer who was willing to take on such a "strange case," I could not afford to pay their fees anyway. In the end, I was forced to face the fact that, on a horizontal level, I was in this battle alone.

Soon enough, the day for the hearing arrived. The judge seated himself with an air of firm resolve and cleared his throat with determination. After preliminary proceedings, he turned to me and asked, "Do you understand why you've been called here today?"

"Yes, sir. The school board superintendent explained everything in a letter. I have a copy of her letter right here," I answered as I handed it (Sony's marks and all) to him across the desk.

He started to toss it aside, but then paused and, after studying the letter at length with keen interest, asked, "Who made these notations on here?"

"I'm very sorry, sir. My daughter did that when she asked to see the letter on the day it came. I felt since it was about her, she should be allowed to know what the letter contained. I was a bit distraught when it arrived and did not notice that she had written on it until the deed had already been done."

"So, *she* made these spelling corrections?"

"Yes, sir."

"She can read and understand this level of writing?"

"Yes, sir."

"And, she is how old?"

"Seven, sir."

"I see. Hmmm." After a few more questions about curriculum and hours spent on teaching, my educational background (or, more correctly, my lack of educational background) and such, he leaned back in his chair and looked at me for what seemed like an eternity.

"Well, although this is highly unusual, based on your answers and the evidence I hold in my hand, I would say your daughter is obviously being educated—and [looking accusingly over his glasses at the superintendent] it is apparently *not* a result of the influence of our public school. It looks as though you are doing a fine job. Keep up the good work. You are dismissed."

At this point, the school superintendent erupted in a tirade not suitable for printing in a Christian book. I walked out of that meeting feeling as if the weight of the world had been lifted from my shoulders! Little did I know that it would not be the last time I would stand in a court room to defend my right to raise my children according to my convictions but, for the time being, we were "home free"!

Many has been the time in my life when I have faced difficult circumstances and found myself utterly unable to find help for the situation from any other human being on the earth. *"Give us help from trouble: for vain is the help of man. Through God we shall do valiantly: for He it is that shall tread down our enemies"* (Psalm 60:11-12).

Most of us think we know countless numbers of people in a variety of contexts—work, church, extended family, neighborhood, etc., but, the way to really get to know someone is to spend time alone with them—to walk side by side with them through the mountains and the valleys of life.

It was in these lonely times of trouble that I learned to draw near to my God Who has promised that, when we do that, He will draw near to us (James 4:8), and through those intense times of close fellowship and communion with my LORD I have found Him to be always faithful, absolutely trustworthy—all sufficient for my every need (2 Corinthians 12:9).

Interestingly, the more I came to know Him, the less I needed or desired human confirmation or affirmation. *"Whom have I in Heaven but Thee? And there is none upon earth that I desire beside Thee. My flesh and my heart faileth: but God is the strength of my heart, and my portion for ever"* (Psalm 73:25-26).

He Who promised, *"I will not leave you comfortless: I will come to you"* (John 14:18) is true to His Word.

When my friends were out of town, or asleep at four o'clock in the morning—or had completely abandoned and forsaken me—I found that I was never really alone *"...for He hath said, I will never leave thee, nor forsake thee"* (Hebrews 13:5). *"God is our refuge and strength, a very present help in trouble"* (Psalm 46:1).

There are times when we realize we are standing alone even when surrounded by friends (Luke 9:18). Yet, sometimes, we are asked to stand alone even in the midst of a hostile crowd (John 8:9).

Thankfully, today, we are enjoying a measure of tolerance toward homeschooling—but tolerance is a world apart from acceptance. The wheels of the antagonists are still turning and every effort is being made to find a way to grind the homeschooling movement into a fine powder that can be blown away with the slightest wind of change. Are we willing to stand on our convictions and faithfully homeschool our children—even if homeschooling isn't cool?

It takes courage to stand alone. Fear is a fierce enemy. When we truly understand that, no matter what the circumstances, the only safe place for us to stand is in obedience to the perfect will of the Lord—even if that means standing there alone—then we will find the courage we need to confidently take our stand for Him, come what may.

"The fear of man bringeth a snare: but whoso putteth his trust in the Lord shall be safe" (Proverbs 29:25).

HOMESCHOOLING AMIDST OPPOSITION

"Yea, and all that will live Godly in Christ Jesus shall suffer persecution" (2 Timothy 3:12).

Homeschooling is one of those issues that remains controversial in today's society. Not everyone will be patting you on the back and singing your praises regarding your decision to take full responsibility for your own child's education.

Rather than fearing the inevitable questions from the curious (and, yes, sometimes downright nosey) folks you will encounter, just accept the fact that inquiring minds *will* want to know "just exactly what you think you are doing keeping those children out of school." Begin to recognize these encounters as opportunities to give an account for the faith that lies within you with regards to Godly parenting, and prayerfully prepare yourself in advance to respond to those questions as the Lord leads.

Sometimes the situation warrants a thoughtful, respectful response as in those cases where the one showing an interest is truly seeking to understand your position. Other times the "question" poses more of an accusation—or even a threat.

A few well-rehearsed lines can get you through even the most awkward situation when faced with opposition from well-meaning family members, friends and neighbors. In fact, I'll loan you a few to get you started:

Your neighbor: "Is homeschooling legal?"

"Homeschooling is every bit as legal as government schooling only it's a lot less hassle, a lot more efficient—and a whole lot more fun!"

Your doctor: "What about socialization?"

"Well, right now the children are all getting their socialization immunizations and it's best that they not be around a lot of other children at this time."

Your in-laws: "What about college?"

"The boys plan to work with their dad in developing our family business so that their cousins will have a place to work when they get their degrees."

Your mother: "When we get to the family reunion, *please* don't mention that the children are homeschooled. Can't you just tell Aunt Sally that they attend a private, Christian school (preferably in a well-to-do neighborhood)? And, did you have to wear that denim jumper?"

(Tip: Whenever two questions are presented with one breath, always ignore one question and answer the one less threatening.) "No, I could have worn my other one."

Now, obviously, we're just funnin' here. You may decide to take my tongue-in-cheek advice but actually, our God, knowing very well what folks are like, has warned us that we will face opposition and has told us exactly what to do in situations such as these:

"But before all these, they shall lay their hands on you, and persecute you, delivering you up to the synagogues, and into prisons, being brought before kings and rulers for My Name's sake. And it shall turn to you for a testimony. Settle it therefore in your hearts, not to meditate before what ye shall answer: For I will give you a mouth and wisdom, which all your adversaries shall not be able to gainsay nor resist" (Luke 21:12-15).

Most of the time, the opposition we face is simply annoying but, more often than we like to think, sometimes it turns downright ugly. This is where we can learn a few lessons from those who have had the unfortunate experience of getting trapped in the nightmare system of Child "Protective" Services.

On a practical level, if you wish to avoid serious trouble, it is imperative that you keep a careful watch over your children at all times. Always know where your children are, what they are doing, and with whom they are doing it.

We know of one homeschooling family who lost all ten of their children to the foster care system for an entire year because one of the children was bitten by a dog while under the care of a babysitter.

In another case, nine homeschooled children were removed from their home when trusted friends convinced the oldest daughter that her family was "weird" for not allowing her to date boys or hang out at the mall with her friends, and encouraged her to "seek help." The "investigation" found the parents guilty of "emotional abuse and neglect" for failing to provide the children with a "normal" upbringing that included all the "benefits" of the government school. After almost a year, the children were returned to the home only when the parents agreed to attend parenting classes and keep the children in the government schools that they had been forced to attend while in the custody of the State.

One homeschooling family was dealing with rebellion and habitual lying in their oldest daughter. Desperate for help, and on the advice of their pastor, they decided to take her to a "Christian" counselor who subsequently uncovered "repressed memories" of abuse involving the father who was immediately arrested, tried and "convicted of the crime" (solely on the basis of the counselor's testimony) and is now serving 15 years in prison. To this day, the daughter has no actual memory of any such abuse having taken place, but believes it "must have happened" since the counselor insists that it did. When the mother refused to divorce her husband (based on her firm belief in his innocence and her first-hand knowledge of her daughter's lifelong lying problem) all the rest of the children were removed from the home and placed in foster care and government schools.

One of the best ways to deal with opposition is to avoid it! Don't court trouble. A commonsense approach to homeschooling is the best defense against becoming an offense. A few practical suggestions for avoiding trouble: Don't go out to the market during the weekdays with the children in tow. Don't be hanging out down at the community playground when the school bus is scheduled to pass by. Don't allow the children to be playing out in the yard during "school hours." Don't be in-your-face rude to those who don't share your enthusiasm for homeschooling or are in any way involved with the government schools.

In other words, there's no need to go out and buy trouble when it is more than ready to come looking for you—free of charge!

Well-meaning friends, relatives and neighbors or, perhaps, misguided, overbearing "professionals" can undermine even the most stouthearted parent, possibly causing undue confusion and discouragement, or instilling deep-seated fear and anxiety.

Everyone needs encouragement from time to time—and homeschoolers are no exception. While some may look to counselors, support groups, and the like, for temporary relief, believe me, there is no better cure for this common homeschool malady than a generous dose of the Word of God!

"Looking unto Jesus the author and finisher of our faith; who for the joy that was set before him endured the cross, despising the shame, and is set down at the right hand of the throne of God. For consider him that endured such contradiction of sinners against himself, lest ye be wearied and faint in your minds" (Hebrews 12:2-3).

Get your Bible and let's turn to Him right now and seek His counsel on these matters…

When doubts and questions flood your mind, where do you turn for answers? (James 1:5)

Do you doubt your ability to adequately fulfill your calling as a homeschool parent? (1 Thessalonians 5:24)

Do you find yourself fretting about all the "what ifs"? What if my children grow up to be social misfits? What if my child fails to measure up to government standards? What if someone decides to make trouble for us? What if…? (Psalm 55:22; 1 Peter 5:7)

So what if trouble does come? (John 16:33) Do you really think that God has called you to burn yourself out trying to please friends and relatives, maintain an impossible schedule, or satisfy the state requirements for academics? (Matthew 11:29)

When the weight of the homeschool load that you are carrying gets to be "too much," perhaps it's time to test that load against His scale (Matthew 11:30).

Unschooling vs. Unit Studies? Phonics vs. sight-reading? Are you confused as to which curriculum/method/approach is right for you? Are you tired of being pulled in all directions? (Jeremiah 6:16)

So, what can a homeschool parent do to ensure the serenity, success and fulfillment of their calling?

Pray (1 Timothy 2:1, 2). Hold fast to the promises of God (Isaiah 32:17,18). Relax (Proverbs 3:5,6)!

As long as you are careful to love the Lord your God, and to serve Him each day with all your heart and soul, then your heart and mind, and your homeschool, can be completely carefree—and "nothing and nobody" will be able to stand successfully against you!

"These things I have spoken unto you, that in Me ye might have peace. In the world ye shall have tribulation: but be of good cheer; I have overcome the world" (John 16:33).

Finding and Giving Real Support

There has been much discussion over the years about the nature of homeschool support groups: Should they be exclusively Christian or open and inclusive of any and all who wish to attend? I would rephrase the question: Should they be "exclusive" or truly Christian?

From what I have observed, the average American Christian is about as deep as a mud puddle and just about as pure. As a result, upon encountering one, the average American pagan has learned to sidestep them on sight. Yet, incredibly, we Christians are so worried about getting soiled by *our* contact with the world!

What are we so afraid of? If we are convinced that we are right in all that we believe, do, and say, then what do we have to fear from someone who supposedly has less light than we claim to possess? If we have the vaccine, then what reason would we have to fear the disease?

The common ground of homeschooling provides a wonderful opportunity for outreach to unbelieving families. Just start with the things you have in common. These folks obviously love their children or they wouldn't be making the sacrifices necessary to home educate them. Plan family activities together. Have a cookout. Make plans to attend a used book swap or homeschooling seminar together. Bake an extra loaf of bread each week for their family. Just look for ways and opportunities to minister the love of God to them in the Name of Jesus. It is a rare individual that will turn away from genuine love!

We need to take steps, personally and corporately, to make sure that our lives are producing substance of such quality that it creates a *desire* in others for that which flows, supernaturally, out of our lives. Like a dying man in a desert longs to find cool, clean, life-giving water, the world should be inexplicably drawn by the undeniable truth of His grace, mercifully at work in our lives.

Jesus did not hide from the ones who did not believe in Him even though *He knew* that they were actually going to put Him to death. Still, He made Himself available. He was not afraid of their questions. He welcomed them. He doesn't want us holed up in our safe house looking out for me and mine—He wants us to go forth. As mature Christians, He has called us to be salt and light—to make disciples.

Jesus does not need us to join His club. Do you think Jesus didn't know that the woman at the well could not sign His statement of faith? A truly Christian Support Group is going to be reaching out to the lost in His Name. Frankly, I don't think Jesus appreciates us tacking His Name on to something that is, in reality and in practice, against everything He lived and died for. I suggest we either change the game or change the name.

You say, "What about the verse that says, 'Can two walk together except they be agreed?'"

Too many people misuse that verse as an excuse to shun or exclude those who do not agree with them on every point. Besides, I've known far to many folks who could sign the most conserative statement of faith without qualm—but despite their alleged doctrinal purity, lived like the devil and were definitely not a blessing to be around.

Friends, it is through Jesus that we find true unity—not in printed statements and creeds. Christ living in you will draw all men unto Himself and, in this way, you will have precious unity and sweet fellowship. True, some will reject us just as they rejected Him. Still, those who are drawn to His Spirit in us will be treasured friends indeed.

Fellowship among likeminded (*Christ*-minded) believers is a precious gift. However, we will only possess this gift with any sense of appreciation when we are ready to lay down our lives (*and* our arrogant high-mindedness *and* our stubborn dogmas a*nd* our selfish agendas) in the selflessness of genuine love and humility, and begin to esteem others as better than ourselves. We must acknowledge our need for one another and value the relationships He brings into our lives.

Do you know at least one other homeschooling family in your area? Do you get together for fellowship on a regular basis? Why not set aside an evening in the near future to sit down and talk about some mutually supportive concepts that you, as parents, can covenant to walk out together in real Christian love? For example…

Walk together in truth. In America, image is everything. Americans work hard at being able to put forth a positive self-image. The majority work harder at trying to *look* successful than actually *being* successful. As long as folks *think* we're cool, we're cool. Tell the truth now—even worse than falling and hurting yourself on a patch of ice, is to know that someone *saw* you fall and make a fool of yourself! Right? The idea is: it doesn't matter if your world is falling apart as long as you can keep the rest of the world from knowing it!

Don't settle for the image of having it all together. Be real. Admit it when things aren't going so well or you've blown it with the children that day. Covenant together to be honest with each other.

Confess your faults to one another. Proverbs 28:13 teaches us that, *"He that covereth his sins shall not prosper: but whoso confesseth and forsaketh them shall have mercy."* Notice, though, that confession is only half the battle. You must demonstrate the ability to turn from those sins, as well. Learn to speak the truth in love—not only to the other person about the other person, but also about yourself!

Covenant together to speak and receive the truth. Whenever truth is *spoken*, if there is going to be any profit gained, it also needs to be *heard*. Covenant together with homeschooling parents who are serious about living as true disciples of the Lord Jesus to report and receive both positive and negative truth about each other's children, whether observed or heard. Be willing to confront each other if it seems there are inconsistencies in actions or lifestyle. Let me give an example of how this type of open, honest interaction might play out in real life.

Scenario #1: Your daughter has long been friends with a girl her age who belongs to your local homeschool support group. The two of them are always looking for any excuse to get together and spend as much time together as possible. This girl is always a blessing to her family and a joy to be around. As usual, at church this morning, your daughter's friend approached you for permission to have your daughter spend the afternoon at her house. However, your daughter has shown some serious signs of rebellion over the last few months. A month ago, she sneaked out of the house for several hours late at night. She claimed she was just "out taking a walk" and yet, her siblings admitted that they had heard her arrange over the phone to meet some friends and go to a party. Just last week you caught her having an inappropriate conversation with a much older boy on the Internet.

How should you handle this situation? You should explain to your daughter's friend, in the presence of her parents, that your daughter is really not in a good place right now, spiritually, and that it really would be risky for them to allow unsupervised interaction with any members of their family. You should not mask the details or cover the nature of your daughter's sin. Your daughter will not appreciate this as it is always more difficult to sin in the light, but it will establish a firm groundwork on which you all can reach out to her in love. Until she has come to full repentance, it is best for all concerned that all social contacts be limited to joint family ventures with adults staying within hearing and seeing range of the young people's activities at all times.

Scenario #2: A new family has moved to your area and you've discovered that they have just started to homeschool their children this year. To welcome them to the community, your family has begun to interact with them on a regular basis. Together, they are a delightful family. However, their middle son seems to have a dual personality. In the presence of his parents, you could not ask for a nicer, quieter boy, but away from authority, to be frank, he is a disrespectful, foul-mouthed bully. Repeatedly, he has been observed punching, shoving, threatening and generally intimidating the younger boys. Once, when you caught him in the act and tried to confront him, he roughly pushed you aside informing you rudely that you are not his mother!

How should you handle this situation? Don't wait for another episode and risk reacting in the heat of a battle—pray about a time to go to both parents and talk to them about what you have personally observed in their son. Assure them that, as a parent, you know that we all face these situations with our children from time to time and that your purpose in coming to them is not to sit in judgment or bring condemnation, but to stand with them and support them in their desire to do their very best for their children. Their boy may have been so good at deceiving them that they will have a difficult time even picturing what you are describing but, with their eyes having been enlightened, they can now be watchful and purposeful in dealing with their son, making continued sweet fellowship with them possible.

Friends, we're not talking about a Gestapo approach to parenting. What we are describing is genuine mercy in action. If you ever have to stand with heartbroken, grieving parents at the graveside of a wayward child who lost his very life because of sin that went unaddressed and unchecked, you will know that it is not kind or loving to "keep your mouth shut" under the guise of "not wanting to interfere." That type of response is the most selfish and cowardly thing you could do.

Running your mouth to other people about the neighbor's ornery children is easy—going to them directly and confronting them with known sin in the lives of their children (or in the lives of the parents themselves) is tough. However, it is the kindest, most considerate,

FINDING AND GIVING REAL SUPPORT 45

most merciful thing you could ever do for them. *"Let a righteous man strike me—it is a kindness; let him rebuke me—it is oil on my head. My head will not refuse it"* (Psalm 141:5). Can you make that statement? Is that a conviction in your life?

A while back we did a seminar in another state. The needs among that group were so great (not that they were unusual in that respect) and the folks were so open to receive the seed we had sown that the group asked us to stay another day. We prayed together and agreed and then continued in prayer for the remainder of the evening.

The second day, we saw folks begin to open up to each other and confess their sins to one another. We were able to witness this beautiful moment as God honored His Word among them and people began to be set free from those things that had so devastated their lives! We still hear from those folks, and the good work that God began among them at that time is still going on to this day!

Love one another. Bear with one another. Let's not just *talk* about loving our brother, let's do it! Talk about a support group! Why waste your time with anything else?

Several years ago, we conducted our *Homeschooling for Eternity Seminar* in the beautiful state of Tennessee—during an excruciating heat wave! At each of my sessions, I had a solitary, but vociferous, heckler. This woman mocked, scoffed, interrupted, and generally disrupted every session with her running negative commentary and outbursts.

"Discipline? That's cruel and inhumane!"

"Accountability? Ridiculous! I TRUST my children!"

"Family togetherness? Nobody lives like that! Besides, how can my children be salt and light if they don't spend time in the *real* world?"

"Siblings showing genuine love and respect for each other? That's just not reality! It's *normal* for kids to fight!"

"Biblically-based homeschooling? The Bible has its place, but I think homeschoolers should stick to *real* books for learning! How else are they gonna make it in the *real* world?"

And, so it went. I was never so glad to end a speaking session!

One year later we were booked to do a seminar in another part of that great state. When I stood up to speak, I looked out over the audience and found myself staring into the all-too-familiar face of my old Tennessee Heckler! Her eyes locked onto mine as she leaned far forward in her seat—obviously ready to pounce!

I swallowed hard, sent up a quick prayer, and began to speak. Sure enough, I'd hardly reached my second point before she was off and running! Just a few minutes into the session, she stopped me mid-sentence and demanded, "Wait a minute!"

"Oh, no! Here we go..." I thought.

With notebook in hand she asked, "Could you repeat the reference for that verse?"

I could hardly believe my ears! With every point that I made, and every Scripture that I quoted, she would interject emphatically, "That's true! She's right! That's exactly how it is!"

At one point, she grabbed the arm of the startled woman sitting next to her and shook her firmly, saying, "She's right! You need to listen to this!"

When I was finished, she stood up and asked permission to address the entire group. She then proceeded to explain to everyone that she had sat in a similar session only a year ago. With tears streaming down her face she began to share the painful events of the past year—how tragedy upon tragedy had fallen upon her family, and had, ultimately, brought her to her knees. Finally, she had opened her heart to the Word of Life that had completely transformed her way of thinking and her life! She urged everyone in attendance not to harden their hearts against the truth and concluded with the words, "If only I had listened when I had the opportunity, my family would not have suffered the things we have endured this past year!"

Astonished, I thought to myself, "Boy, we need to take this lady with us on the road!" Without any manipulation on my part, my former antagonist had become my biggest fan!

The moral of that story is this: don't be so quick to write off those who are not "like-minded." Not everyone is at the same place. Don't feel like everyone has to be standing exactly where you are on every issue. The fact is, not everyone will agree with you on every issue. Just be in your place. Speak and walk in truth. Serve your brothers and sisters without judging them. Let God be God!

If you have established your purpose and practice in gathering together as being totally, unwaveringly Christian, and those who are not of like faith are willing to come under that umbrella and open their hearts to your ministry (regardless of whether or not they can, in good conscience, sign your statement of faith at the outset) reach out in faith in the Name of Jesus and win them for the Master.

Establishing God's Order For Your Homeschool

When it comes to homeschooling, most of us have encountered the skepticism of family, friends, neighbors—and even strangers at the grocery store! But, what if the contention lies within your own household? What if your spouse does not bear witness with your desire to accept full responsibility to train up your children under your own roof?

Like it or not, the fact of the matter is that God has established the proper order and function of the home and we would do well to stop fighting against the will of the Lord on this matter and simply find our place and get in line.

What is God's order for the home? Husbands are to gently lead. Wives are to follow and support. Children are to obey. What do we not understand?

HUSBANDS AND FATHERS ARE TO GENTLY LEAD

"Husbands, love your wives, and be not bitter against them" (Colossians 3:19). *"Husbands, love your wives, even as Christ also loved the church, and gave Himself for it; That He might sanctify and cleanse it with the washing of water by the Word, That He might present it to Himself a glorious church, not having spot, or wrinkle, or any such thing; but that it should be holy and without blemish. So ought men to love their wives as their own bodies. He that loveth his wife loveth himself. For no man ever yet hated his own flesh; but nourisheth and cherisheth it, even as the Lord the Church"* (Ephesians 6:25-29).

What if the wife is reluctant (or adamantly opposed to the idea) to homeschool? Or, what if she sincerely longs to teach the children at home and the husband is against it?

There is never a reason for a husband and father to bully his family ("Because I'm the man and I said so, that's why!") on any issue. Since the husband represents Christ in the home, the wise husband will do well to ponder and prayerfully consider the humble example of the Savior. *"He shall feed His flock like a shepherd: He shall gather the lambs with His arm, and carry them in His bosom, and shall gently lead those that are with young"* (Isaiah 40:11).

In the same way, husbands are to give honor to their wives. Rather than commiserating with his carnally-minded buddies about how they "just don't understand women," the Godly man knows how to live together with his wife in an understanding way (1 Peter 3:7). The wife may be physically weaker than her husband, but she is his equal partner in God's economy. Together, they must lay down their fears, preferences, and agendas and fervently apply themselves with open hearts and minds to seek and to do the will of the Lord.

Too many fathers are content to "just let mom handle it" when it comes to homeschooling and child training, but it is *fathers* who are commanded to bring up their children for the glory of God. *"And, ye fathers, provoke not your children to wrath: but bring them up in the nurture and admonition of the Lord"* (Ephesians 6:4).

The home is not the woman's realm alone. I've heard husbands say, "The home is her domain—me, I just stay out in the shop (or the barn, or at the office)." However, when addressing the role of a bishop our God clearly stated His expectations for those Godly men, *"This is a true saying, If a man desire the office of a bishop, he desireth a good work. A bishop then must be blameless ... given to hospitality* [In the home? Isn't that women's work?!] *apt to teach ... One that ruleth well his own house, having his children in subjection with all gravity; For if a man know not how to rule his own house, how shall he take care of the church of God?"* (1 Timothy 3:1-5). (Actually, I've often wondered that myself. Why would anyone want to take their children to sit under the teaching of a man who refuses to obey God's Word and teach his own children? Just a thought…)

The same high standard was held for deacons. *"Let the deacons be the husband of one wife, ruling their children and their own houses well"* (1 Timothy 3:12).

You may be a farmer, or a pastor, or a corporate executive but it is clear from these passages which define the characteristics of truly

Godly men that God expects a man to discipline and teach his own children and to rule his household well.

WIVES ARE TO FOLLOW AND SUPPORT

"Wives, submit yourselves unto your own husbands, as unto the Lord. For the husband is the head of the wife, even as Christ is the head of the church: and He is the Saviour of the body. Therefore as the church is subject unto Christ, so let the wives be to their own husbands in every thing" (Ephesians 6:22-24). *"Wives, submit yourselves unto your own husbands, as it is fit in the Lord"* (Colossians 3:18).

Wives who are not openhearted about taking responsibility to educate their children at home can undermine their husband's attempts to rule his household well by constantly whining and complaining and pretending that God (through the husband) has placed on them more than they can bear. This is nothing more than an attempt to manipulate the husband by wearing him down until he comes around to her way of thinking.

"The aged women likewise, that they be in behaviour as becometh holiness ... teachers of good things; That they may teach the young women ... to love their husbands, to love their children, To be ... keepers at home ... obedient to their own husbands, that the word of God be not blasphemed" (Titus 2:3-5).

Playing the role of the suffering saint is not true submission. The Godly wife will wholeheartedly serve and support her husband's decision to homeschool. The flipside of this picture is the husband who absolutely will not allow the wife to homeschool. If the husband is wrong, the Holy Spirit is more than capable of showing him the error of his ways—and protecting the children during the interim. Meanwhile, the wife has a responsibility to carry out, in a cheerful and supportive manner, the plan her husband has established for the home. If he insists that the children must be placed in school, rather than wringing her hands in despair, she must rally every fiber of her being to cover the children to the best of her ability, redeeming every moment spent with them and praying all the while that God will have mercy on them all and change the heart of her husband on this matter.

"Likewise, ye wives, be in subjection to your own husbands; that, if any obey not the word, they also may without the word be won by the conversation of the wives; while they behold your chaste conversation coupled with fear" (1 Peter 3:1-2).

CHILDREN ARE TO OBEY

I've heard children harangue their parents to allow them to attend the government schools and I've also heard children rant and rave and beg their parents to teach them at home. Despite the desired outcome, neither approach is acceptable.

"Children, obey your parents in the Lord: for this is right. Honour thy father and mother; (which is the first commandment with promise;) that it may be well with thee, and thou mayest live long on the earth" (Ephesians 6:1-3).

"Children, obey your parents in all things: for this is well pleasing unto the Lord" (Colossians 3:20).

In the context of the home, any member at any level has the right (and, in some cases, the obligation) to respectfully appeal to one or more members of the household who stand in authority over him/her with regards to decisions that are being, or have been, made. Once all the issues have been presented and discussed, the person presenting the appeal has a responsibility to accept the decision of the party in authority to whom they have appealed without further debate. To continue repeating oneself in order to try to sway the decision maker is to invite argument and stoop to participation in the unprofitable works of darkness that will only create discord and strife. Remember, you can always carry your appeal directly to the Highest Power Who promises always to hear and to work in your best interests!

EVERYONE IN THEIR PLACES

As with the genuine and, at times, excruciating discomfort of physical pain, emotional distress is not something to be taken lightly. Prolonged emotional trauma can even tempt us to believe the erroneous assumption that our God has not kept His promise to withhold from us more of a burden than we can bear. However, based on the truth of the Scriptures and my own experience with the eternal God, I can assure you that is never the case.

So, why do these painful situations sometimes occur and what can be done about them?

Disunity in the home is sure to create an atmosphere ripe for the development of emotional overload. Quarreling between parents and/or siblings will drain the life right out of your homeschool efforts. These often arise when there is disagreement between parents about such issues as financial matters or how to raise the children.

No matter what the issues, don't let things get to the point that you've all got the "screaming meanies!" Unity in the home is of the utmost importance if you are expecting God to bless your homeschooling efforts. See that Godly order is established with everyone in their place and playing by the rules. Then, take a day off (or even a week if necessary) to sit down and talk things out and set some guidelines and come to some agreement.

Parents are often exposed to undue pressure from well-meaning (or, just plain nosey) friends or relatives who are "concerned" about the "lack of socialization" or the quality of education the children are receiving. You've got to learn to shake that stuff off. A lower emotional pressure level allows everyone to better gauge the situation and to respond appropriately.

Stop being a people-pleaser! If you are going to make it for the long haul in homeschooling, you must refuse to allow anyone or anything to create an emotional overload and carry you away into bondage. Always refer back to that tried and true Litmus test—our God told us that "His yoke is easy, and His burden is light." If you are feeling weighted down as a result of your decision to homeschool, you have, more than likely, allowed someone to dump something on you that God, Himself, would not ask you to carry. It may be a standard, or a tradition, or an image, or a false assumption, or feelings of fear, guilt, or inferiority. Whatever it is—and before it totally shipwrecks you—you must do a little serious inventory and toss that stuff overboard by ruthlessly ridding yourself of anything that does not pertain to life and Godliness! When the Lord sets you free, you will be free indeed—and you are going to LOVE homeschooling!

God established this homeschooling process for your own good. As you disciple your children, the Heavenly Father is discipling you. How many times I've found myself dealing with something in one of my children and all of a sudden I realize that the reason I'm so familiar with this sin is because it's in ME! It's *my* weakness. They've probably heard me spouting it or seen me do it! So, while they are in their room praying through on that thing, I have to head for my room to pray through on the matter as well! I'm crying out to God right along with them and saying, "God, do this work in me, first. Don't leave me like this. I don't want to be one of those 'do as I say, not as I do' kind of folks. I don't want to just tell them what they should do, I want to model Jesus for them. I want to show them how to get the victory over this." That is God's plan—that we will *all* continue to grow in the knowledge of our Lord and Savior. Amen?

THE BITTER FRUIT OF DISORDER

One of the most prominent problems we encounter among parents in general is their expressed ineffectiveness in dealing with anger—both in their children and in themselves. When emotional issues are not swiftly and effectively dealt with, underlying bitterness and resentment that boils over into unrestrained anger is almost inevitable. This problem will manifest itself in the form of disunity and discontentment, bickering and arguing, misplaced aggression, and even physical violence.

They key to deliverance from such a state is complete surrender to God in every area of your life. You can only become "upset" if there is something remaining in your heart that stands against the will and way of our Lord. If each day you are asking Him to order your steps, then anything that comes your way that day will be viewed not as an interruption to your plans but as God's divine purpose and plan for your life. Some of what comes your way has been allowed there so that you can take dominion over it while some things that you will face must simply be accepted as that which cannot be changed. If you have surrendered your life completely to His will, then nothing can unsettle you from the quiet confidence that is your inheritance as you walk each day resting in His peace.

Likewise, if you have given yourself in absolute obedience to His Word and His way, there will be no inner turmoil and conflict between the spiritual and the carnal nature. You will approach each day as an obedient child of the Father with no other agenda than to please Him. This is a life that our God can bless. When you find peace of heart and mind in this manner, nothing and no one can disturb the deep-seated joy that will be consistently characteristic of your life—no matter what circumstances you face. It is in this way that you will mirror and impart Christ-likeness to your children—and to the world around you.

What is more important—to achieve academic success, or to nurture children who faithfully grow and mature into the full stature of His image?

You do not have to be a slave to anger. By His grace, you can refuse to ride that emotional roller coaster. The more you are able to get hold of these truths and apply them daily to your approach to homeschooling, the more you will find yourself being set free from the chains that have kept you bound for so long. Are you ready to relinquish control of your life, submit to God's order in all your relationships, turn over the keys to your emotional prison and experience that deliverance and freedom that only the Christ can give? Are your ready to truly let Jesus be LORD of all—including your home *and* your homeschool?

Your homeschool will be a clear reflection of the quality and spiritual condition of your home life. You can't expect to have peace and harmony in your homeschooling endeavors if you have not first attained it in your home. Open, honest communication in an atmosphere of love and humility is of the utmost importance in the Godly home.

"...be ye all of one mind, having compassion one of another, love as brethren, be pitiful, be courteous: Not rendering evil for evil, or railing for railing: but contrariwise blessing; knowing that ye are thereunto called, that ye should inherit a blessing" (1 Peter 3:8-9).

This God-ordained order for families is foundational to any successful homeschool. To attempt to homeschool on any other foundation is to foolishly build on the shifting sands of humanism. Our God is a Master Builder Whose glorious work will remain standing throughout all eternity. You'll never go wrong when building by His design. *"Except the LORD build the house, they labour in vain that build it: except the LORD keep the city, the watchman waketh but in vain"* (Psalm 127:1).

Finding Hope at the End of Your Rope

Through the years, I've gotten many letters and phone calls from people who feel they have "reached their limit." Through a series of events, life has become overwhelming for them and they are finding it hard to face each new day. Often, after pouring their hearts out in frustration, they will invariably end with the comment, "Of course, you wouldn't understand." I always laugh! Oh? Wouldn't I?

Years ago, before I knew Jesus as Lord, I found myself facing abandonment, eviction, and the prospect of life alone, while shouldering sole responsibility for feeding and raising six children, ages 1, 2, 3, 5, 11, and 13. The accumulated strain of recent years had left me in seriously poor health complicated by impaired mobility. As a high school drop out with severe dyslexia, and no real formal education beyond the ninth grade, my prospects for landing a job that would alleviate my desperate financial situation, and pay for a babysitter while I was away at work, were slim.

Job's comforters were always at my door with helpful suggestions—"Well, there's always welfare." "You really should put the kids in foster care." "You're in no shape to work as hard as you do and try to raise these children by yourself. You'll kill yourself if you keep on going like you are."

Despair was becoming my constant companion. It seemed that I was hopelessly trapped with no way out. I felt like my life was a waste and that I was of no use to anyone.

Now, that which I had greatly feared was coming to pass—I was alone again bearing the stigma of rejection and failure known as divorce. Not that life, in reality, was going to be any more difficult for us than it had been in the years leading up to that point. Humiliation, poverty, homelessness, violence, and abuse had been our everyday reality. Still, I had become rather familiar with the navigation of those murky waters and, strangely enough, any kind of deviation from that miserable existence was uncharted and unknown and, therefore, *even more frightening* to me.

Fears assailed me from all directions—what was I going to do? How would I ever be able to provide for the children? How could I possibly juggle managing a household, while filling the role of breadwinner and continuing to homeschool in the process? Surely, I would have to put the children in the government school, and go out and try to find a job—and, was the latter even possible considering my lack of formal education and physical limitations?

Then, there were the sobering statistics from various agencies predicting impending doom for children raised in homes without a father. According to the doomsayers, I may as well go look for a house next door to the prison so that I could visit my children often once they had reached adulthood! That bleak picture may have become a reality were it not for one startling event that changed the entire course of my life.

I was a fixer—a people-pleaser by nature—and had literally worn myself out from the years of trying to keep peace, fashion some sort of decent home life, make ends meet, and raise the children in the process. Day in and day out I was driven beyond reason to make things work out somehow. After a particularly devastating series of events, the stark reality stood before me uncloaked and unvarnished. Slowly the verity was beginning to dawn on me that there *are* evil people in the world—and I was married to one of them! Gradually, as I stared those demons in the face, I just felt incredibly tired and hopeless. The years of physical abuse and intense emotional stress had taken their toll. I increasingly dreaded the thought of each new morning's dawn and the burden of having to face another day. Eventually, I decided that, all things considered, suicide really was the most merciful option for the sake of everyone concerned. I simply could not go on any more living the bleak existence that had become my life.

One evening, after the children were all asleep, I made up my mind to carry out my plans to solve my problems once and for all. Calmly, I finished straightening the house and then sat down to write a list of final instructions for my oldest daughter. Occasionally, I would stop writing to search the recesses of my brain to see if I could come up with any other options. I could not. Was there any other way out of this misery? There was not. *Finish the note. Get the gun. Do what you gotta do.*

My plan was to try to get far away where no one would know me so that the children would never have to know the awful details of how it ended. With the gun hidden under my coat, I reached to turn out the last light before heading out the door.

An electric-like shock shot through me as a gentle, but insistent, voice broke through my troubled thoughts, "WAIT!" I looked around, heart pounding. I saw nothing, still it continued. "I love you. I can help you. There is a ram in the bush. I've got so many wonderful plans for you. Things can be different from now on. Won't you let Me show you how beautiful life can be?" Well, I'd heard that line before and I wasn't about to fall for it again. *No thanks—I ain't buying.* The pleading continued. "But, you really don't know Me. You've never given Me a chance to show you what life would be like if I was in control." He knows my thoughts! Who is this? Could it be God? *Keep talking. You've got my attention.* "I've been here all along and I know all about your sins and your struggles. I've been waiting for you to turn to Me. Stop trying to work everything out in your own strength." *I have no more strength. I am literally at the end of my rope. I cannot live another day like this.* "Then, there's hope! You can trust Me." *Everyone knows what a mess I've made of my life. Even my friends call me "the eternal screw-up"—and it's true. I'm tired of seeing my children suffer because of me. How do I know this is You and not just my brain playing cruel tricks on me?* "You can trust Me. If you will let Me, I will live for you, in you, and through you every day for the rest of your life. Just trust Me. You don't have to do it alone." *I want so much to believe. There is just the tiniest part of me that believes that I really can trust You. But, I know me. It is ME that I don't trust. Please—help me, Lord.* I began to weep.

For the next four hours, I had no more words of my own. I could only pour out my pain in a river of tears while He spoke words of promise, faith, and hope to my weary heart. As I emptied out the sad and sordid contents of my broken heart, He filled it with a calm, quiet peace and a life-giving hope. Finally, with my hand in His, He lifted me to my feet and we took the first faltering steps toward walking this road of life together—with Him in the lead! When the dreaded morning came, it dawned full of the light of faith and I knew beyond a shadow of a doubt that life would never be the same.

As my fears came to pass and another self-serving man walked heartlessly away from my life, Another took his place—but there was something different about this One. This One said (as had the others) that He loved me. As I knelt with Him at the altar, this One promised (as had the others) to never leave me or forsake me. He promised (as had the others) to provide for my every need, and protect me from harm, and to be a Father for my children. My friend, I want you to know that, from that day to this, *not one word of His promises has failed* and we have walked this road of life together ever since.

So it was, that I met the God of the universe and came to know Jesus as the Lord of my life and the Savior of my sin-burdened soul! It is all because of Him that I have been able to overcome adversity and accomplish anything worthy of mention or having eternal value. He turned the painful darkness of my past into brilliantly sunny days of walking confidently and peacefully in the joyous light of His love. Maybe you think I'll never get done bragging on Him, but when you really get to know Him you'll understand—you just can't help but love a God like that!

If this is not your reality, then cry out to Him from the depths of your heart today! I promise you that He is real, and He is a rewarder of those who diligently seek Him (Hebrews 11:6). Don't settle for a life that is less than glorious when this very day can be the start of a whole new way of living. Shake off the chains of your past—no matter how heavy they be—and begin to walk in victory toward a wonderful new life. If you're at the end of your rope *just let go!* Fall fearlessly into the waiting arms of Jesus and I promise you that He will carry you through.

Comfort and Advice for Single Parents

Those of us who have experienced the grief and anguish of divorce probably understand like no one else can just why our God says He hates divorce. There is nothing you can do about yesterday—but because His mercies are new every morning, the possibilities for today are endless! You can choose to live your life in the shadows as "So-and-So's Ex," or you may step into the light of His grace and stand, as His precious bride, firmly planted in the place to which He has brought you—as a joyful mother of the children which He has entrusted to your care.

If the children's father or mother refuses to listen to reason or be governed by Biblical principles and has decided to leave, the Bible says, let them depart. LET GO! Stop begging and pleading and chasing them. Stop threatening them and trying to manipulate and control them. Obey the Word—release them! Give every fragment of your shattered heart wholly to God and get on with the business of living for Him.

Absolutely refuse to take on victim status. No matter what the details of the past, the future is in your hands. From here on out, if you continue to make a mess of your life you've got no one to blame but yourself. It's time to take full responsibility for your own actions. Admit the fact that, while you may not have played the starring role in your personal little soap opera, at the very least, you played a supporting role. Repent for your part in the sins of the past and turn every bit of it over to the One Who has the power and authority to wipe your slate clean! Relinquish control and leave it in His capable hands. With God in control, I promise you, *things will be different!* You'll find that

His plans for you are nothing but good! Remind yourself often that His mercies are new every morning (Lamentations 3:22-25). Determine to rise each day with thanksgiving in your heart for the opportunity He has given you to experience a wonderful new life—better than anything that you could have ever imagined or accomplished according to your best laid plans.

Put bitterness behind you and don't look back. Forget those things that are behind and press forward (Philippians 3:13,14). Allow God to fulfill His good promise to restore the years that the locusts have eaten (Joel 2:25). Get a life!

That doesn't mean you should start scouting for another marriage partner, by the way. You'll never find the joy and peace you are longing for until you stop looking around the planet for another human being who can meet your needs, fulfill your longings, and fix what is wrong in your life. Such behavior is an insult to our God Who stands ready, willing, and able to provide, and to *be*, all that you will ever need in this life. So many single or divorced people leave Him waiting in the wings while they spend countless wasted hours fantasizing about some Romeo or Juliet out there in LaLa Land. The abundant life He longs to give remains an unopened package while precious days, weeks, hours and years are spent in mourning over the spiritual graves we insist on digging. Meanwhile, who's minding the children?

No matter what your former spouse does or does not do, you have a responsibility to the children. Stay focused. If your marriage and divorce was traumatic, then the children will need your undivided attention all the more. Thank God that you now have the opportunity to invest yourself fully, and without distraction, in the lives of your children. By the grace of God you can build a firm foundation under their feet and provide a nurturing habitat in which you all can grow close to each other and your God.

Don't allow guilt, or the feeling that the children have "suffered enough" through the painful process of the divorce (and, possibly even during the marriage) to cause you to be lenient with them in areas where you need to be tough. Many parents indulge themselves in permissiveness toward the children in a misguided attempt to *win* the children over to their side by being a *buddy* rather than a parent. The absence of one parent does not necessitate the absence of Godly order in the home.

If your former spouse remarries, and the children are forced to divide their time between households, don't give in to the temptation to relax the standards of your own home in order to compete with all the cool stuff, exciting entertainments, and various enticements strategically employed to lure their allegiance away from you (and God) and over to the other parent.

Faithfulness and consistency based on Biblical principles will go a long way toward establishing a solid relationship with your children that will not easily be shaken. Much healing takes place when the peace of God reigns unhindered in your midst. When just a little girl, my youngest came to me one day asking, "A lady at church said that us girls come from a broken home. We're divorced, but our home's not broken. We used to be broken, but not anymore!" Out of the mouths of babes! There's no sense of lack when Jesus is held in honor as the head of a household.

Learn to look to Jesus, and Him only. People can only do so much, but Jesus can do anything! People will fail you, but Jesus will never fail. Stop worrying. God has made very specific promises to widows and orphans. Trust Him and stand on His Word. You are in Good Hands!

When it comes to the practical aspects of providing the physical necessities for the family, always think in terms of pulling together rather than drawing apart. The "work from home" possibilities are endless as long as you are flexible and creative.

Home business options can provide apprenticeship opportunities for middle and older children, which are both provisional and educational. The children can have the satisfaction of knowing that they are a contributing part of the family rather than a burden. Responsibility develops strong character. There is no better preparation for the "real world" than hands-on participation in real situations under the guidance of a loving parent!

You may need to rethink your priorities and adjust your concept of what it means to make "a living." Particularly in this country, people can get by with so much less than what they think they need! If it is truly your desire to homeschool your children, then you must be willing to do whatever it takes to accomplish that goal. If it becomes necessary to downscale, *do it!* If being able to homeschool the children under your roof means yard sale clothes, dented cans and stale bread, and no entertainment budget or luxuries such as eating out at restaurants (or maybe even a smaller roof) *so be it!* What a small price to pay for the privilege of being together as a family and the blessing of walking in obedience to the Scriptures!

When approached properly, homeschooling is such a simple, natural process! Generally speaking, the classroom model does not fit in the homeschool setting over the long haul—especially in the single parent household. It is not your job to personally try to impart every morsel of knowledge to each individual child. Rather you must seek to set up a well-balanced educational buffet and then call them to dinner! Your children will need to be equipped and taught how to learn, and then properly motivated to pursue learning on their own initiative.

To eliminate the daunting task of the traditional annual ritual of selecting new textbooks each year (for each child!), begin to track down real-world resources (encyclopedias, dictionaries, grammar guides, reference books, etc.) which constitute a one-time investment that will serve them throughout their lifetime.

So, how can one person simultaneously accomplish all that is required of a single, homeschooling parent?

The art of multi-tasking (learning to do two or more jobs at the same time) will enable you to accomplish all that is set before you in a day's time but, hey—in the event that you are unable to get it all done today—there's always tomorrow!

Be realistic about how much you can accomplish in a day. Don't spread yourself too thin trying to do all things for all people. Understand what it is that our Lord has specifically ordained for you to do and then do it to the best of your ability and with all your heart in the reasonable time He has allowed.

In our case, in the beginning, I didn't have a clue as to how we were going to survive financially. As I began to take stock of the situation, some of the only things I knew for sure were, 1) I believed with all my heart that God had given me six children to raise for His glory, and homeschooling, in my estimation, was not an *option*—it was a mandate! 2) Since there was no one to go out and "bring home the bacon," I needed to find some kind of work that I was physically capable of performing, that would enable me to stay at home and take care of my first priority—my children. 3) After all the Lord had done for me, I wanted the remaining years of my life to count for some eternal good.

All I knew to do was go to the Lord and pour out my heart to Him. When I read in the Word that He promised to give us the desires of our hearts, I told Him that my desire was to homeschool the children for His glory and not have to leave them with a sitter while I went out and worked eight hours a day for someone else. I read in the Bible where someone prayed that God would not make him so poor that he would steal nor so rich that he would forget Him, and I made that my prayer as well. When I read that He intends for us to work six days and rest on the seventh, and that He wanted the first-fruits of His provision to be returned to Him, I promised to be faithful to do both.

I prayed fervently and unceasingly. Oh, how I prayed! My faith and commitment to everything I believed in was tested to the very limit! However, the very things that seemed like impossibilities to me at the time, became strong points and, in the long run, proved to be an integral part of God's provision for our every need. Against all odds, I made a decision to hold fast to that which I knew the Lord had called me to do, committed my ways to Him, and waited for Him to direct my path as He had promised. (Proverbs 3:5,6.) I was not disappointed.

Over time, an idea began to form in my mind that turned out to be (I realize now, with hindsight) the call of God on my life to a very specific kind of work. As a mother of six, and one of the unwitting "pioneers" of the homeschool movement, parents would often seek me out for counsel and advice on education and parenting matters. Over and over, I would force myself to turn away from my own personal problems and reach out to these struggling young parents who were searching for answers and practical help on raising Godly children. Eventually, I felt that I needed to get some basic homeschooling/parenting information into a printed format that I could simply distribute as a means of helping these families.

I spent some time at the local newspaper and quick print shop, and drove those good folks bananas by watching closely over their shoulder and asking a million questions as they tried to go about their daily tasks in each department. With some searching and persistence, I acquired a typewriter (a computer was way out of my budget range!) and typed out, pasted up, and distributed our first 32-page homeschooling newsletter.

In those early days, it was a lot of hard work making important contacts on the phone and typing manuscripts and address labels on my old manual typewriter—always with two or more toddlers or nursing babies on my lap! I would begin each day by getting up long before the children in order to read my Bible, pray, start laundry, fix breakfast, and line up their scholastic assignments and chores for the day.

In my line of work (printing and publishing), most of my duties could be interrupted at any point so I was usually available to the children and was always listening or watching for those moments when they required my hands-on ministry or input. Throughout the day I maintained an "open door" policy in the little area I had designated as my "office" with the understanding that, if the children wanted to read or talk with me, or show me something they had made or done, they could come in and see if I was free at the moment—or at least at a good stopping point.

If I was busy on the phone temporarily, the children knew that they were to go back to their activities and try again a little while later. Or, they were to stand quietly by and wait patiently until we made eye contact. As soon as I was able to get off the phone, I would go looking for that child so that we could spend a few moments together over whatever they wanted to share with me. If it was important or an emergency, they were to come to my side and whisper quietly to alert me to any pressing needs, in which case, I could merely excuse myself from the conversation and attend to the family issues at hand. Every hour on the hour, I made the rounds to check on them and spend a few minutes talking about anything they wanted to discuss or instructing them.

In the evenings, unless we were facing a press deadline, I tried to pull away from the office work and spend some concentrated time with the children. Once they were all settled in bed for the night, I would go back to work and tackle those things requiring the greatest concentration and undivided attention, such as writing or editing.

In order for this type of set-up to work, balance is the key. The biggest challenge for me has always been to fully focus on whatever I was doing at the moment without feeling guilty and thinking I should be doing something else—whether it was working and feeling like I should be with the children, or being with the children and feeling like I should be working!!

I'll confess that I asked my God on a daily basis to order my steps and guide me through each decision I made every hour of every day. I knew that if I stayed in the center of the road He had mapped out for me that I'd be headed in the right direction and wouldn't end up in the ditch with mud on my face (or His)!

I remember the day when we reached two hundred subscribers—I could hardly believe there were that many people in the world who were interested in what we had to say!! I was sure they had all *meant* to subscribe to another magazine and had accidentally addressed the envelope to *Home School Digest* instead!!

But, you all know the rest of the story. Ultimately, the Lord used our desire to serve others to open doors for us to minister to homeschooling families around the world. Today, that little 32-page newsletter has grown to nearly 100 pages and has been read by tens of thousands of folks! The Lord has abundantly rained down blessings on our family and ministry!

Life is not all roses—but at least there *are* roses! I could hardly have believed, in light of our dire circumstances just a few short years ago, that we would ever see the deepest desires of our hearts come to pass. Since most of the children participate full time in our family ministry, we have the blessed privilege of working together as a family to help others to fulfill their God-given responsibility to bring their children up in the nurture and admonition of the Lord through homeschooling. Who would have ever believed that He would bring us out of the muck and mire of the past, and establish us in such a *large* and fruitful place? Here's the best news of all—that same God is ready, willing, and able to do the same for *you*!

Don't ever think that just because there is no father (or mother) in the home, the whole thing has to crumble. The husband is not the foundation upon which we build—Jesus is the only sure foundation on which to base our hopes for the future. He has a tender spot in His heart for widows and orphans (the husbandless and fatherless). He will be your strongest support.

"Behold, the Lord GOD will come with strong hand, and His arm shall rule for Him: behold, His reward is with Him, and His work before Him. He shall feed his flock like a shepherd: He shall gather the lambs with His arm, and carry them in His bosom, and shall gently lead those that are with young" (Isaiah 40:10,11).

Homeschooling In Sickness and In Health

Far too many families assume that homeschooling becomes impossible when long-term illness or infirmity strikes the home. However, health challenges do not automatically necessitate placement of children in the government schools. God will not call you to face a task that He will not also equip you to perform. He can enable you to stand strong in the Spirit even when you lack the physical or emotional strength to get out of bed!

I can tell you that, in many ways, I discovered that it was actually easier to homeschool during times of infirmity because I was not able to be up and running as usual. When I was down in one spot I could spend concentrated amounts of undivided time with the children. I was not distracted by housework or chores but could give the children my full attention. A side benefit in all of this was that their presence and the close fellowship we shared during these times was a comfort to me which mercifully distracted me from the pain or general discomfort of my affliction.

When it comes to sickness, I will confess that I have had my share (and, sometimes I think possibly someone else's share!) of physical challenges. But, since nobody likes to sit and listen to the gory details of anybody's long list of ailments, I will forgo a recital of my own troublesome circumstances and share with you, instead, this inspiring true story of an exemplary homeschooling family who have suffered through the realities of debilitating physical ailments and overcome them to be able to continue homeschooling by God's grace.

When Bobbi and Dan* married back in the mid-1980s, they weren't so sure they really wanted to have children. Slowly, God began to open their hearts to receive children as a gift from Him and, together, they made a commitment to receive as many children as He would see fit to bring into their home.

A sweet little daughter was born into their home followed, a year later, by another precious baby girl. When their third child, a son, was stillborn at seven months into the pregnancy, the pain of that loss was acute. So, they were excited to learn that another child was on its way into their world—only to suffer disappointment once again as a third little daughter was born hydrocephalic and left them the same day she arrived. Though badly shaken, soon they rejoiced to learn that Bobbi had conceived once again. In the stillness of the night, each of them battled paralyzing fear even as they anticipated the arrival of their infant child. Once again, a bitter reality crushed their fragile dreams as another son joined his siblings cradled in the arms of Jesus.

With empty arms and full heart Bobbi continued as the keeper of their little home to homeschool, nurture, and train their two small daughters while shouldering devastating grief over their profound loss. So, it was with mixed emotions that Bobbi felt the first twinges of morning sickness as she went about her daily routine. Could she really go through this again? The alternate longing and disappointment were almost more than she could bear. But, her mother-heart could not completely close to the desire to glorify God in the precious stewardship of more children so Bobbi continued to hold fast to the God of her salvation as she awaited the outcome of yet another pregnancy.

Meanwhile, God spoke to Dan's heart and said that this child was a boy. He assured him that he was fine and that his name was to be Joshua. And, true to His Word, this time, their faith was rewarded here on this earth with a blessed gift to heal the pain of their multiple losses. It was, indeed, a beautiful baby boy. He was fine. And, they named him Joshua. And, it wasn't long before another son was added to this little homeschooling family. Two boys and two girls—their joy knew no bounds!

Following a dinner and time of fellowship together at our home, we learned that Dan and Bobbi were soon to be blessed with yet another child. I smiled at the thought, having observed in each one of their children the pleasant result of effective, Godly homeschooling. But, a shadow once again passed over this precious family when, during her seventh month of pregnancy, Bobbi learned the dreadful truth that she had cancer. How we praised God (and cried out to Him for mercy) when, just a few weeks later, baby Janet was born—beautiful, healthy, perfect!

Immediately following the birth, in what they, themselves, have described as "a panicked frenzy," Dan and Bobbi's search for a cure for the parasitic disease that Bobbi now carried in her body led them to leave the children temporarily behind here in the States and travel a considerable distance to an alternative treatment clinic. However, the hoped-for cure proved to be less promising that the hype and, many weeks later, the sad couple returned home. Local believers gathered up the children to meet them at the airport and welcome them home.

Upon leaving the airport, Dan rode in the back with the children. While both parents and children had eagerly anticipated this reunion, it looked as if it was going to be brief. Along the way, during the long ride home, Dan took the opportunity to explain to the children the seriousness of the situation. Although he was trying to be brave, tired from the journey and weary of the battle, despite his brave efforts, he suddenly lost composure and broke down and wept. The driver of the car later shared that he was sure he was hearing an angel choir when out of the dark, there arose a sweet, strong refrain. It was the voice of one of the children rising up as a candle held high and shining brightly in the incredible darkness of that night, singing:

"How firm a foundation, ye saints of the LORD,
Is laid for your faith in His excellent Word!
What more can He say than to you He hath said,
To you who for refuge to Jesus hath fled?
Fear not, I am with thee—O be not dismayed,
For I am thy God, I will still give thee aid.
I'll strengthen thee, help thee, and cause thee to stand,
Upheld by My righteous, omnipotent hand.
When through the deep waters I call thee to go,
The rivers of woe shall not thee overflow.
For I will be with thee, thy troubles to bless.
And sanctify to thee thy deepest distress.
When through fiery trials thy pathway shall lie,
My grace, all sufficient, shall be thy supply.
The flame shall not hurt thee—I only design
Thy dross to consume and thy gold to refine.
The soul that on Jesus hath leaned for repose,
I will not, I will not desert to his foes!
That soul though all hell should endeavor to shake,
I'll never, no never, no never forsake!"

What a powerful testimony!

Just a few days later, we buried the body of that precious homeschooling mother after she had graduated, with honors, into the presence of the Lord Who had, indeed, been her firm foundation—only four short months after learning of the cancer.

Now, Bobbi was not perfect. She made mistakes. But, in the time she had here on this earth, she applied herself wholeheartedly to being a wife to her husband, a mother to her children, and a friend to all she met. She had her priorities in order. She equipped her children for the future, and, she finished her race victorious! Now, having gone on to be with the Lord, her children, though not yet even ten years old at the time of her death, by the fruit of their little lives, had already risen up to call her "Blessed."

I am confident that, if Bobbi were here writing this today, she would assure you that the application for entrance into heaven does not contain any math or science questions! Therefore, my advice to you is this: homeschool your children as if the only test you are really concerned about passing is the Ultimate Test—the one with eternal consequences.

Homeschooling is not just an option—in a very real way, it really is a matter of life and death. Don't assume that you have plenty of time to get around to teaching your children the things that are important. Approach every homeschooling day as if it were your last.

"And whatsoever ye do, do it heartily, as to the Lord, and not unto men; Knowing that of the Lord ye shall receive the reward of the inheritance: for ye serve the Lord Christ" (Colossians 3:23-24).

(**Names and minor details have been changed to protect the privacy of the family.* Dan, by the way, has courageously continued to homeschool the children while working from home in the years since Bobbi's home-going.)

Educational Challenges

All my life, I believed that I was stupid. In fact, at school, that became my middle name—STOOPID! (My first name was, HEY.) It still echoes in my mind as painfully loud and clear as it did in the school corridors, "Hey, STOOPID!" All my siblings had perfect grades and borderline genius IQs while I flunked out of everything but music year after year. Everything that came so easy for them was extremely difficult for me. In order to get by, I literally begged, borrowed, bribed, stole or otherwise cheated to get the answers I needed to make me look good on paper. I was the original "fake it till you make it" kid! Finally, my brother broke the "news" to me that I was adopted and that certainly did explain some things—until I got to be a good bit older and looked in the mirror one day and saw my father's (and my grandmother's!) face staring back at me!!

The year that I entered ninth grade, our little school consolidated with several neighboring schools and along with that major change came the introduction of "guidance counselors" into the school program. The stated purpose for these highly credentialed individuals is to aid the student in discovering their strengths and weaknesses according to areas of natural interest and abilities, and to direct them into the appropriate vocation which best utilizes those aspects of their character and personality.

Finally, the day for my consultation arrived and I nervously took my seat on the other side of the counselor's desk. Slowly and methodically, the counselor "guided" me through the list of all the things in which I was, obviously, *not* excelling. All the colleges were looking for top-honors students, he explained, and all the students were looking for grants and scholarships (which required top grades). When I countered that I was fairly good at music and that I seemed to do better than most at counting money in my head, he noted that since most businesses utilized cash registers (a trend he felt would undoubtedly continue) and I was not exactly what you would call technologically savvy, the likelihood of getting a job as a cashier was slim to none. Since I flunked Phys. Ed., he seriously doubted that I would even have the poise and coordination to even land a job as a waitress down at the local truck stop. Since I was basically self-taught in the area of music (sight/note-reading being another difficulty for me) and played mostly by ear, and since it was not likely that I would get any kind of scholarship based on those qualifications, he strongly advised me to stop wasting my time—and theirs—and just drop out of school.

I am sitting here shaking my head now as I recall that I actually thanked him before I left his office that day and promptly followed his advice. It wasn't until my oldest were teenagers that I came to understand the learning challenges that I have struggled with my whole life.

In 1965, a drastic shift in the focus of education from academics toward behavior modification took place when the Elementary and Secondary Education Act (ESEA) opened the door to federal funding to schools for—not teachers—but social workers, psychologists, and psychiatrists. Since that time more than 7,000,000 children within the government school system have been labeled, registered and treated as patients. Interestingly, in the United States, increasing numbers of boys between the ages of six and fourteen have been "diagnosed" with ADHD. Had I not homeschooled my children, my son would certainly have been caught in this insidious web.

ISRAEL'S STORY

Israel began walking and talking at about eight months. Walking was no problem, but talking was another matter. Not that he was shy. (Those of you who have met my son or heard him speak publicly would never buy that story!) No, he was quite ready and willing to talk anytime of day or night to anybody who would listen. Understanding what he was saying was another matter. His sister, being two years older, was the first to consistently comprehend and decode exactly what he was trying to say and continued to hold her position as his official interpreter for several years thereafter. The reason he needed an interpreter is because he stuttered. He was so eager to communicate that his words just came tumbling out in a terribly broken and jumbled mess that would have to be painfully and strategically deciphered.

Meanwhile, those first toddling steps toward walking quickly gave way to climbing (on the roof), running (away with strangers at the mall), jumping (into trouble at every turn—with both feet!), and every kind of mischief imaginable! My mother kept assuring me that it was just a stage he was going through. Keeping Israel alive during this "stage" required one full-time mom ("Where's Israel?"), one full-time big sister ("I wouldn't do that if I were you, Israel!"), and several full-time guardian angels drawing generous amounts of overtime pay.

Fortunately, with persistence and patience, we were able to completely overcome the stuttering problem, but the hyperactivity continued long after he was finally able to tell me *why* he did whatever it was that he had just done—even though he knew he was not supposed to do it.

There was nothing wrong with his brain, I can assure you. Still, I knew we were in for a joyride when I introduced his very first math lesson.

"Okay, Israel, let's see if you know the answer to this problem. If Billy has two apples and Johnny has none, how many apples are there altogether?"

With deeply furrowed brow, he searched deliberately for the answer before he slowly replied, "Well, if Billy has two apples (pause) and Johnny has no apples (very long and thoughtful pause)—then why doesn't Billy's mama make him share?!"

Israel was always *thinking*. In fact, usually when he was in trouble it was because he had been "thinking" about something—and decided to follow through on those thoughts. However, when he was *supposed* to be thinking about something (school lessons, for example) he could not concentrate on the subject at hand for more than 10 seconds at a stretch!

"Israel, look here in your science book on page…"

"Wow! Did you see that yellow bird out the window?"

"…and, why are all these pages from yesterday's assignments still blank?"

"Hey, Mom! How do you like the neighbor's new kitchen curtains? By the way, what are we having for lunch?"

"But, son, you just had breakfast an hour ago! Now, pay attention!"

Such was the rhythm of a typical homeschooling lesson with Israel. Not that the lad was without talent—even as a young boy, he was extremely creative and resourceful, and could operate and explain the workings of just about any electronic gadget in the house. Of course, a lot of perfectly good watches, radios, stereos, and small appliances had to lay down their lives on the altar of hands-on learning in order for him to gain this commendable status.

LEAVE IT TO THE PROFESSIONALS?

At a certain point in the children's education, prior to my coming to know the Lord, I was facing seemingly insurmountable odds at various levels and feeling quite overwhelmed. As a result, I gave in to the relentless pressure to place the children in the local Christian school for a year believing it to be, as everyone insisted, the "best thing for all concerned."

Still, I was determined to stay involved in their education as much as possible. Day after day, I would quiz the children when they would come home from school.

"So, what did you learn in school today, Sony?"

"Oh, we studied about ..." and off we would go for quite some time running through the gamut of courses that filled their classroom day.

"How about you, son? What did you learn in school today?"

"Nothing." (Silly me. I thought he was just being evasive.)

But, before long, I began to notice a highly interesting phenomenon unfolding before my ears and eyes. As Sony would start to detail the events of the day, Israel (who had learned "nothing" in school that day, mind you) would begin to develop muscle and bones in his limp, slumped-over body. Hardly able to wait his turn without interrupting, he would become increasingly animated and verbose as he interjected excitedly into Sony's narration to relay those aspects of the day that had obviously held his interest.

"...and then in Science class—" Sony would begin.

"You wouldn't believe the big knife Randy brought to school today!"

"Knife?! I thought the guidelines said no knives in school."

THE EDUCATIONALLY CHALLENGED   73

"Yeah. The teacher took it away from him and he had to stay inside for recess so he missed out on the fight!"

"Fight?! I thought the guidelines said no fighting on school grounds."

"Yeah. Wow! You shoulda seen it! But Sony shoulda plugged her ears 'cause after Steve punched him in the nose, Billy said that bad word again."

"What word—NEVER MIND! I thought the guidelines said bad language would not be tolerated in school."

"Yeah. Anyway, I'll betcha Billy won't ever try to steal Steve's cigarettes again."

Stealing? Cigarettes? Far from learning "nothing" my son was getting quite an education!

The fact of the matter is, for Israel and others like him, the classroom setting often provides an overwhelming distraction to already overloaded brainwaves. The excess stimulation of classroom activities coupled with the antics of other bored classmates can shove any chance for real learning right out the window!

As you will recall, I was pressured into placing the children into school that year because it seemed that it would be "the best thing for all concerned." My daughter had done reasonably well, academically, having continued to apply herself as she had done in her private studies. However, interestingly enough, when my son was tested again at the end of that school year he actually tested *one year behind the level he had been at when he entered that school.*

So, in essence, after that year's grand experiment, we found ourselves, officially, two years behind. Of course, the teachers wanted to blame this on my son's "learning disability" (ADHD). He needed to be on medication, they said. Well, that makes sense. Let's face it. What self-respecting professional teacher is going to admit that they have a "teaching disability" when the politically-correct thing to do is to label every failing child as a disabled learner?! It didn't take another year to decide that maybe, in reality, it would be the "best thing for all concerned" for us to homeschool after all! Never again would I doubt my ability to adequately and effectively teach my own children—despite the most challenging of circumstances!

It wasn't until Israel was in his early teens and I was now teaching his younger sisters as well, that I came to realize that he and Mercy were encountering some of the same problems when trying to read that I had faced my entire life. It was also around this time that I became aware of that masquerading deceiver called dyslexia.

Suddenly, the light came on. Watching several of my children struggle to decipher text and add or carry numbers in columns on a page was like reliving my childhood education all over again. Let me describe a little of what it was like…

Simple things were always painfully frustrating for me. Letters jump around on the page and words transpose themselves right before my eyes. Trying to look up a number in the phone book was torture. If I did not check, and then double check, and then check one more time just to be certain that the name on the left really was directly across from the number on the right, I would end up talking to an irate stranger on the other end of the line who would confirm what all the kids at school had already pounded into me—I was STOOPID!

When it came to math I was utterly hopeless. All those columns and rows of numbers and decimal points floating around on the page refused to cooperate so that I could calculate them into any logical conclusion. The only thing that ever worked for me was to try to convert the numbers to monetary denominations in my head. (For some reason, I could always count money and make change!)

The advent of calculators did little to alleviate my distress as I have always been quite technically challenged, as well. Trying to dial the phone was (and is, to this day) always a multi-attempt endeavor. Anything with a numerical keypad requires extreme focus and concentration. Comprehension and retention of information is attained with great difficulty—the moment I look away from something I am trying to copy, it is absolutely *gone*. And, typing—well, some of you were wondering why it took me so long to get this book finished?!?

I tell you this not to sing the blues and cry on your shoulder, but so that you will understand even just a little bit of what it is like to live, and try to function, with dyslexia. Possibly, you recognize one or more of your own children in this description—or, maybe even yourself!

Dyslexia, ADD, ADHD and other challenges to learning are simply that—*challenges*—hurdles to be tackled and overcome. They are not a death sentence to your future dreams or goals. There is no need to mask or hide the fact that you or your child may face one or more barriers to learning or functioning. Most likely it will mean that your approach to learning or performing a task will differ from others. So be it. In a world of individuals, isn't that true of most of us?

For example, most dyslexics are auditory learners. Therefore, much of the hindrance to understanding what is read can be overcome by learning to read aloud. If you continue this pattern for any considerable length of time, you will note dramatic and rapid improvement in the level and ability of the reader.

While technology can be a good thing, don't let electronic gadgets replace actual working-knowledge and true comprehension. The calculator and the spell checker might *cover* your ignorance, but they will never help you to *overcome* it.

My father worked and taught in the Tool and Die industry for 50 years. He often remarked that the young men who were graduating from the schools with a paper in hand claiming they are competent and skilled in their trade, really had no concept of reality with regards to the actual outworking of their projects. If they misapplied their formulas or miscalculated the figures on their little hand-held brain, they had no systematic grid by which to compare the numbers shown against the reality of the final product. However, in the Tool and Die industry, being even slightly off on one's calculations can result in a pinhead-sized project turning out so large that it would have to be chopped in pieces to allow it to be transported on our nation's highways! Merely memorizing formulas is not enough to ensure success. Possessing a vital comprehension of a subject is imperative for achieving "expert status" in any field. No theoretical degree can replace hands-on learning and an active working knowledge of one's subject.

Incidentally, although my father taught for many years at the college level, he never attended college as a student or possessed a degree in higher education. He is a classic example of a self-educated man who applied himself to his trade with initiative, ingenuity and integrity. As we heard over and over at his retirement gathering a few years ago, anyone who ever worked with my father will tell you that he was truly an expert in his field—not to mention being a gifted teacher, ingenious inventor, and talented musician besides.

Most importantly, as the parent of a child who possessed none of his positive attributes or skills, my dad (and my precious mom—neither of whom ever understood what I faced in school mainly because I was too embarrassed to let them know) always encouraged me to keep trying and just do my best, and loved me equally even when the best that I could muster was far below the capabilities of my brainy and multi-talented siblings. No matter what challenges a child may face in life, there's just no replacement for the power of encouragement found in the enabling love of a mom or dad.

Tuning the Strings of Your Child's Character

In order to see Godly character established in the hearts of your children, you must be focused and purposeful in your approach to parenting. One thing you need to understand at the outset is that you cannot attain a goal that you haven't set. Or, to put it another way, you cannot reach a standard that has not been clearly and previously established. So, how do we determine which standards are right for our home? By what measuring stick do we evaluate our child's character? When it comes to goal-setting, there is no higher standard than that which has been set forth in the Word of our God.

Anyone who has ever set out on a trip with a carload of children knows that children are, indeed, goal-oriented. "Are we there yet?" "How much longer until we get there?" In the same vein, children like to know where they are on the road of life. A clearly defined set of moral standards becomes the road map that will keep them on the right path and help them to achieve Godly maturity all the way through to adulthood.

That is why it is so important to start *now* to train your sons and daughters. Start when they are toddlers by teaching them that "No!" is not just a word you came up with to cramp their style. It is, in fact, a complete sentence—with a period (or exclamation point) on the end. Don't allow your children to spend the first part of their life learning bad habits that will shorten the vital part of life that remains.

Let's just take a few minutes to consider the following as it pertains to the development of Godly character: The Tongue.

Mouthing off to your parents is a good way to trim a few years off your life: Our God has warned us to, *"Honour thy father and thy mother, as the LORD thy God hath commanded thee; that thy days may be prolonged, and that it may go well with thee, in the land which the LORD thy God giveth thee"* (Deuteronomy 5:16).

Mouthing off about other folks can have the same negative effect: The Bible clearly admonishes us, *"For he that will love life, and see good days, let him refrain his tongue from evil, and his lips that they speak no guile: Let him eschew evil, and do good; let him seek peace, and ensue it"* (1 Peter 3:10-11).

"Keep thy heart with all diligence; for out of it are the issues of life. Put away from thee a froward mouth, and perverse lips put far from thee" (Proverbs 4:23-24).

Quick as a flash, all kinds of evil thoughts just seem to come out of nowhere. But, when you begin passing heavy judgments, you're standing on shaky ground!

"So speak ye, and so do, as they that shall be judged by the law of liberty. For he shall have judgment without mercy, that hath shewed no mercy; and mercy rejoiceth against judgment" (James 2:12,13).

"For with what judgment ye judge, ye shall be judged: and with what measure ye mete, it shall be measured to you again" (Matthew 7:2).

To put it another way, there will be no mercy for you if you have not been merciful to others, but if you have been merciful, then God's mercy toward you will win out over His judgment against you!

"But I say unto you, That every idle word that men shall speak, they shall give account thereof in the day of judgment" (Matthew 12:36).

The reality of the situation is that there are probably twice as many folks who are guilty of thinking such thoughts as there are those who actually have the audacity to speak them! So, are the folks who only think such things any better off in God's eyes?

"For as he thinketh in his heart, so is he" (Proverbs 23:7). Jesus came *"that the thoughts of many hearts may be revealed"* (Luke 2:35).

FACING THE MUSIC

Even if you seem to be avoiding the consequences of your actions so far, *"Ye have sinned against the LORD: and be sure your sin will find you out"* (Numbers 32:23).

You may think that what you have said about someone "in confidence" will "not go any farther" but, eventually, someday, your sinful failure to control your tongue will be brought to light. *"For there is nothing covered, that shall not be revealed; and hid, that shall not be known"* (Matthew 10:26).

God knows every thought and hears every spoken word. Since He is carefully weighing your words in order to prove what measure of man (or woman) you really are, shouldn't you be diligent to do the same?

"Either make the tree good, and his fruit good; or else make the tree corrupt, and his fruit corrupt: for the tree is known by his fruit. O generation of vipers, how can ye, being evil, speak good things? For out of the abundance of the heart the mouth speaketh. A good man out of the good treasure of the heart bringeth forth good things: and an evil man out of the evil treasure bringeth forth evil things. But I say unto you, That every idle word that men shall speak, they shall give account thereof in the day of judgment. For by thy words thou shalt be justified, and by thy words thou shalt be condemned" (Matthew 12:33-37).

No matter what our age, our deeds reflect our true character and the real condition of our hearts. *"Even a child is known by his doings, whether his work be pure, and whether it be right"* (Proverbs 20:11). This is why it is absolutely imperative that you know each child's character strengths and weaknesses, and deal with them accordingly.

GETTING TO THE ROOT OF THE PROBLEM

Someone said to me once, "You talk about these things as if they were a matter of life and death!" Well, to be honest with you, Godly character *is* a matter of life and death—both in this life and in the next. If you think you can live like the devil down here and then be transformed into an angel up there, you're in for a real surprise!

A child that cannot humble himself to submit to you, as a parent, will not be able to submit to others, or to surrender his life to God.

Just think very carefully about each one of your children. Don't rush through this process—take time to really consider each one of your children with regards to each character trait listed below. (This is by no means an exhaustive list—the issues presented here are just a few thoughts to get you started.)

Actions are born out of—and indisputably reveal—the character that lies buried deep in our hearts. If you have a child that is hateful, bossy, vindictive, quarrelsome, angry, destructive, selfish, greedy, lazy, prideful, boastful, arrogant, dishonest, deceitful, untrustworthy, disloyal, or unloving, then he does not possess the holiness that reflects the character of our God. Consider the following actions and what they reveal about those who do such things.

Destructive (vs. Creative) ... does not treat his things or the property of others with care and respect ... tears people down with his words rather than building them up ... gossips or slanders (or tattles on) others rather than concealing a matter in love in order to protect the reputation of another.

An inflated sense of self will never see others as better (Philippians 2:3). It will not value or respect anything that does not originate from itself. The insanity of unbridled SELF is one of the most destructive forces known to man.

Hateful, Vindictive, Cruel, Quarrelsome, Angry (vs. Loving, Peaceable, Reasonable) ... loves to see the other children get in trouble ... enjoys taunting other children ... is merciless in his dealings with others ... blows up, sulks, pouts, bullies, threatens/terrorizes others.

We all remember that Cain sinned when he killed his brother, Abel, but we sometimes forget that several serious transgressions on this list preceded the sin of murder.

Laziness (vs. Initiative) ... waits to be told what to do ... wastes time in idleness and daydreaming ... always looks for a shortcut or pawns his work off on others ... has an endless list of excuses as to why he was unfaithful.

A lazy person has about as much initiative as an echo. A lack of initiative is rooted in laziness. If our God were lazy He could not have created this whole earth in just six days! If we are going to reflect His character, we need to get up and get going—figure out what needs done, and get on with it—and to teach our children to do the same!

Selfishness, Greed (vs. Generosity) ... always runs to be first in line ... wants the biggest and best for himself ... is unconcerned about the needs of others.

Jesus is the ultimate example of selflessness. *"Greater love hath no man than this, that a man lay down his life for his friends"* (John 15:13).

Prideful, Boastful, Arrogant (vs. Humble) ... puts others down in order to build himself up ... scorns humble servitude but craves the limelight ... sees everyone's faults but his own.

The Bible says, *"Let another man praise you, and not yourselves."* Consider this: if our God had meant for us to be patting ourselves on the back all the time, He'd have fixed us up with a different set of hinges at the shoulders. Try it with your children and see for yourself! (I'll warn you though, the older you get the harder it gets to try that little trick.) In the long run, it's what we learn *after we know it all* that really counts. We would do well to remember that our God hates the proud, but gives grace to the humble (1 Peter 5:5).

Dishonesty, Deceitfulness, Untrustworthiness (vs. Truthfulness, Sincerity, Dependability) … attempts to cover his sins with lies and excuses … only tells half the story or completely fabricates a story line … shifts blame and refuses to "come clean" even when caught in the act of wrongdoing … must be vigilantly watched and constantly checked up on.

A boaster and a liar are first cousins. A good parent always knows when their child is lying and will hold that child's feet to the fire (figuratively speaking, of course!) until the whole truth comes to light. If you're having a bit of trouble telling the difference sometimes, here's a little test: truth can stand on its own and never requires a crutch. If it limps, even a little, you can know for certain it's a lie.

If you want to train a boy to grow up to be a man of integrity who can be depended on to never go back on his word, you must not to let him get away with going *around* it either, even a little bit, when he is young. He must learn to let his "yea be yea" and his "nay be nay". He should stand firmly and confidently on the simple truth. A truly successful man, who is known for his integrity, will never be found living on the wrong side of the facts. A Godly man speaks the truth—without embellishment or apology.

Do you imagine your child as a leader one day? Then, deal with his character while he is young! A child who is not afraid to face the music, has the potential to someday lead the choir. Your child will never reach his full potential until he can stand spiritually naked and unashamed before the Lord under the revealing light of truth.

"And this is the condemnation, that light is come into the world, and men loved darkness rather than light, because their deeds were evil. For every one that doeth evil hateth the light, neither cometh to the light, lest his deeds should be reproved. But he that doeth truth cometh to the light, that his deeds may be made manifest, that they are wrought in God" (John 3:19-21).

GOD'S SCALE

If you have a child that manifests these and other negative character traits, don't kid yourself, he simply does not possess true holiness that reflects the shining character of our God. That is why in order for us to truly understand the requirements of our God and be able to impart them to our children we must, first of all, truly know Him.

Don't think for a minute that, somehow, you can pass all this on to your children without first possessing these things yourself. In order to train a child in the way he should go, the parent needs to set the example. The best way to make sure that a child gets safely headed down the straight and narrow path is for you, as a parent, not to draw a map or to give verbal directions, but to *lead them*.

You need not worry (especially those of you who have children who are getting up into the teen years) that you won't be able to teach them. What you don't know, you can learn. Once you've taught them to read they can learn just about any subject on their own. Unlocking the door of their minds is easy enough. But, more importantly, *you* hold the key to their hearts—a key that they will, one day, have to place in the Hands of the Lord Jesus Christ if they are to share a blessed eternity with Him.

It comes built in to every child—from the earliest years when, both physically and figuratively, they "look up" to us as their parents, a standard of measure is established in their little minds and hearts. They begin to absorb, and imitate, every word and deed—they want to be just like us! Just as surely as the moon reflects the sun, those little shadows will someday clearly reflect the values and standards of those whose lifestyle and worldview they have emulated and embraced. *"A student is not above his teacher, but everyone who is fully trained will be like his teacher"* (Luke 6:40).

If we have only a vague idea of what God requires of us, and His clear direction for our lives, and the lives of our children, how can we possibly succeed in our calling as homeschooling parents? *"Can a blind man lead a blind man? Will they not both fall into a pit"* (Luke 6:39b). To ensure ultimate success, our standard of measure must be the same as that of our God. *"For with the measure you use, it will be measured to you"* (Luke 6:38b).

Regardless of how far advanced our children may be academically, or how efficient our record and grading system, human standards will always fall short of God's standards. *"We do not dare to classify or compare ourselves with some who commend themselves. When they measure themselves by themselves and compare themselves with themselves, they are not wise. For it is not the one who commends himself who is approved, but the one whom the Lord commends"* (2 Corinthians 10:12,18).

As parent/teachers, our goal should be to equip the learner for His service within the context of His Kingdom. For the Christian parent, according to God's standard, the most effective outcome of teaching is *"to prepare God's people for works of service, so that the body of Christ may be built up until we all reach unity in the faith and in the knowledge of the Son of God and become mature, attaining to the whole measure of the fullness of Christ"* (Ephesians 4:12,13).

How can we be certain that our children will be able to "make it" in the "real world"? By finally rejecting the lie that worldly knowledge will bring success and, instead, by believing the Word of God!

"His divine power has given us everything we need for life and Godliness through our knowledge of Him who called us by His own glory and goodness. Through these He has given us His very great and precious promises, so that through them you may participate in the divine nature and escape the corruption in the world caused by evil desires. For this very reason, make every effort to add to your faith goodness; and to goodness, knowledge; and to knowledge, self-control; and to self-control, perseverance; and to perseverance, Godliness; and to Godliness, brotherly kindness; and to brotherly kindness, love. For if you possess these qualities in increasing measure, they will keep you from being ineffective and unproductive in your knowledge of our Lord Jesus Christ" (2 Peter 1:3-8).

Many parents vainly try to escape responsibility by admonishing their children, "Do as I say, and not as I do!" This is an exercise in utter futility, because ultimately, the child is not merely going to listen to what you say. When the grown child begins to search out his way in the world, he may have your words ringing in his ears but, by default, he's likely going to follow your footsteps. Verbal, academic instruction alone is insufficient to guarantee genuine success in life.

"Do not be deceived! God is not mocked! That which a man sows, that shall he also reap" (Galatians 6:7). In order to truly *"train up a child in the way he should go"* (Proverbs 22:6) you, Mom—and you, Dad—must show them the way.

There is no sweeter sound than to hear that my children are walking in truth. Just as some musicians learn to play by ear, once you understand God's standards and principles, building Godly character in children is as simple and natural as humming a tune! If we will just be faithful to walk in love, and to hear and to do all that He has commanded us, someday we will hear those wonderful words, "Well done, thou good and faithful servant!" Those are the words that I live to hear—and that, dear friends, will truly be music to my ears!

BIBLICAL DISCIPLINE

How do we "train up" the child in the way he should go? First, we must diligently instruct and guide them at all times.

"And thou shalt love the LORD thy God with all thine heart, and with all thy soul, and with all thy might. And these words, which I command thee this day, shall be in thine heart: And thou shalt teach them diligently unto thy children, and shalt talk of them when thou sittest in thine house, and when thou walkest by the way, and when thou liest down, and when thou risest up. And thou shalt bind them for a sign upon thine hand, and they shall be as frontlets between thine eyes. And thou shalt write them upon the posts of thy house, and on thy gates" (Deuteronomy 6:5-9).

Secondly, we must discipline them. It used to be that if a boy couldn't bring himself to settle down and learn at his mother's knee, he would quickly find himself over his father's knee. There was once a time when, if a child misbehaved just to get attention—he definitely got it!

Nowadays, folks are afraid to spank their children, either because they've swallowed a poison-filled dose of child psychology nonsense, or because they fear repercussions from the Department of Social Services.

Problems arise because too many parents wrongly consider use of the rod as a primary method of teaching. The parent may even say (usually, in anger), "I'm gonna teach you a lesson!" as they prepare to administer this form of discipline. However, there is a whole lot of teaching and training that should take place before the rod of correction ever needs to be brought to bear.

A little boy that I know very well had begun his formal education at about the age of four. His mother rounded up all the preschool workbooks she could find and sat him down each day to study with his older sister. This young lad absolutely loved "doing school" as he called it, and would beg to do "just one more page!" He had seen his parents make notes in books and he would sit by the hour and scribble and draw in the pages of *his* workbooks.

Unbeknownst to his mother, one day he decided to "make a few notes" in his father's expensive new Bible. Unfortunately, the deed was discovered right in the middle of the Sunday morning church service where his father was a pastor. Right there and then, in front of the entire congregation, the boy was informed, in no uncertain terms, that this deed would certainly *not* go unpunished. After the service and all the way home, the railing and threats continued as the boy squirmed uncomfortably in the back seat and stared back, wide-eyed, at a pair of cold, angry eyes which glared at him in the rear-view mirror.

Once home, and barely inside the front door, the punishment began. Upstairs and down, his screams almost completely drowned out by the verbal outpouring of his father's rage, the poor boy was whipped without mercy with his father's belt, despite his mother's pleas. Finally, his anger spent, the father threw down the belt and stomped off to his study as the boy crumpled to the floor in a heap.

Shortly thereafter, his mother tiptoed in to check on her son and found him huddled in the corner sobbing quietly and still struggling to regain a normal breathing pattern. Wanting not to undermine her husband's authority, yet wishing never to witness such a traumatic scene again, she took the boy comfortingly in her arms and said, "Well, son, did you learn anything in all this?" Still unable to talk, with tears in his eyes he looked up at his mother and nodded emphatically. After a minute or two, the mother ventured again, "What did you learn, son?" With a voice brimming with the conviction of a lesson truly learned, the lad replied, "Don't *ever* make Dad mad!"

What kind of lessons are you teaching your children?

The rod is to be used as a corrective measure *only* when the rebellious child is not opening his heart to respond to the training that has already been (and is being) given. Take a minute and read that line again and really let it sink in. If proper training is taking place on a regular and consistent basis, the rod will rarely be necessary.

However, in the face of direct disobedience or outright rebellion, after and despite your faithful efforts to teach and train your child, you must obey God and should not hesitate to use the rod.

"Chasten thy son while there is hope, and let not thy soul spare for his crying" (Proverbs 19:18).

"Apply thine heart unto instruction, and thine ears to the words of knowledge. Withhold not correction from the child: for if thou beatest him with the rod, he shall not die" (Proverbs 23:12-13).

Our God has explained to us that foolishness is bound in the heart of every child (yours and mine are no exception!) but He also has made a simple provision for solving that problem—He tells us, *'the rod of correction will drive it far from him"* (Proverbs 22:15). Who are you going to believe on this matter—carnal-minded "experts" or the God Who made you and before Whom you will ultimately stand one day to give an account of all that you have done in this life? I warn you, if you think you are smarter or more merciful than God, and don't heed His clear instruction in this matter, as a parent trying to navigate the churning waters of child-training, you definitely will find yourself "up creek without a paddle"! (Pun intended.)

A child who does not have a proper fear of the natural consequences of his actions, will usually fear the application of the rod. Of course, there are exceptions to every rule. Some children, though admonished repeatedly to avoid dangerous situations, simply do not fear the consequences of which they are being warned.

When my only son, Israel, was just three years old, he loved to draw pictures of houses. Sometimes, they were single-story dwellings, sometimes they featured a majestic two-story layout. Every house always had lots of windows with trees and flowers growing in the yard under a blue sky warmed by a big, happy yellow sun. The pictures were so charming, that is, until he added the final touch on every drawing—his trademark intense circular scribbling over every inch of the walls of the house—never on the windows, or the trees or the grass or the sky, but *always* covering the walls of the entire house. One day, just as he getting ready to "finish" his beautiful picture I tried to gently intercept it.

"Israel, see how nice this picture looks? Why don't we just leave this one like it is instead of scribbling all those lines on it?"

"Mom, that's the 'lectric wiring! You can't have a house without 'lectric."

"Oh."

By the time he was about four or five years old, he had an insatiable curiosity about electricity. I was always finding scorched bobby pins, paper clips and other such goodies hanging out of the electric sockets. Once, when the circuit breaker blew (again) I heard a loud "thump" and went running down the hall to find Israel lying sprawled out on the floor, melted screwdriver in hand, against the opposite wall of the room in which he had just tried to "fix the 'lectric"! Being greatly relieved to find him miraculously alive, and thinking that this time, surely, he had learned his lesson, I decided to forego the lecture and simply said, "So, Israel, what do you have to say for yourself?" He shook his head and blinked his eyes, looked at the smoking socket, then down at the melted screwdriver, then at me and said, "WOW!"

Sensing that he was missing the point, I pressed on. "Son, if you try that trick again you may very well end up dead! If you *do* live through it, you are going to get a big spanking!" He gazed off into the distance as he pondered the weight of my words, then looked me directly in the eye, reached out and grabbed my hand, shook it emphatically and said, "Deal!" (Needless to say, that was not exactly the response I was going for!)

Israel got lots of spankings—meaning one or sometimes two swats for most offenses, with the most serious offense drawing three. My personal reason for establishing this pattern was to eliminate any possibility of crossing over into abuse due to disciplining in uncontrolled anger which is never justified under any circumstances.

As I went about my housework, if the children were playing outside, I always kept a watch out the window to be on the alert for any situation that may arise, so that I could call the children in and deal with things immediately. In fact, it became such a routine part of our day, that one morning after we had breakfast and the children were headed out to the backyard to play, Israel gave me a hug and said, "Mom, can I have my spanking now so I don't have to come in later?" (Somehow, he seemed to be missing the point!)

One night after a particularly trying day, as I tucked him in to bed, I spent quite some time making sure he knew he was loved, sharing with him how precious he was to me, and telling him what a big help he was becoming to me. We talked of how much fun he and his sister Sony had playing and doing things together, and how he was her only brother and how she just thought that he was the greatest, and what a blessing he is and how sad our little family would be without him.

It wasn't long after that, while engaged in a rowdy neighborhood game of softball, that he noticed (apparently for the first time), the power lines running to the meter which was connected to the outside of the house. As I stood drying dishes where I could watch the progress of the game taking place outside my kitchen window, I noticed

BIBLICAL DISCIPLINE   87

that he seemed distracted and wasn't really paying attention to the game despite the fact that it was his turn at bat. Suddenly, he threw down his bat and, running out to the outfield, grabbed Sony by the hand and dragged her into the house. Wondering what was up, I met them at the door where he caught my hand and led us both to the living room couch (where we usually had our little "chats"—often with the rod applied for emphasis). Seating us both on the couch he said, "I don't want you to be sad so I need you to pray for me because something keeps telling me to touch that big 'lectric on the house and I don't want to do that anymore."

In Israel's case, spanking just seemed like a totally fair and reasonable consequence for the actions of a lifestyle that he fully intended to go right on living. Although he definitely did not want to "get really, really dead" (as he described it) even the fear of death was not enough incentive to keep him from yielding to temptation. However, he wanted very much to please his mama, and to make his sister proud of him, and his tender heart never wanted to make anyone sad. Ultimately, by strengthening these seemingly unconnected, but positive character traits, the victory was won!

Sometimes we train by positive reinforcement. Sometimes we train by restraint or negative consequences. So what's the bottom line on child training? *The wise parent knows which end of the child to pat, when.*

Knowing Your Child By Heart

I am alarmed at the number of homeschooling parents who don't really *know* their children. Unfortunately, there is no patent formula—no one-size-fits-all methodology for child training.

For the child, educational boredom mainly results from arbitrarily using uniform textbooks and workbooks as the main learning tool. Sitting around working on forced, rote memorization of facts that have absolutely no relevance or application to contemporary life is a complete waste of time. Even if they can regurgitate all that stuff back to you at the end of the day or the week—try checking them in a month! They'll probably say something like, "Did we study this? Are you sure we went over this part?" Just because you can cram anything into your head temporarily, that doesn't mean you actually *learned* something.

Many of us have been guilty at some point of creating boredom by employing the following method: incorporation of the classroom model into the home setting as the main method of teaching. This merely creates an artificial learning environment and stymies the potential of the home learning environment. Sometimes, it seems that the best learning takes place when the child is utterly unaware that learning is taking place!

Ask your children what was the highlight of their educational experience last year. I can almost guarantee you that they will never say, "Oh, man! Chapter 14 in my Science book!" If they're having a hard time getting to sleep some night, I can almost promise you they don't lay in bed wishing they could get up and do fractions or algebraic equations!! Truth be known, they may be laying there wishing that you'd had time to talk with them that day because there's something that's really bugging them and they just need your advice or understanding. Children greatly need meaningful activities and interaction.

Incorporate as much hands-on, practically applicable educational opportunities as possible. A boy can study the *Chilton's Auto Repair Manual* until the cows come home but until he gets the chance to lift the hood and lay hands on that engine, the light of understanding won't really come on. A big part of learning is doing. Direct the majority of learning opportunities to those areas that have immediate use or application—or, at least the probability of future benefit.

The study of History is a case in point. Government schools will mark you as a failure if you cannot correctly answer their questions regarding the minutest historical facts, (including such matters as the founding of this country, the Boston Tea Party, the signing of the American Constitution, the names of Presidents and the order that they served, etc.). However, they could care less if you are conversant about historical events that far precede U.S. History—the names and birth orders of the Biblical Patriarchs, or the circumstances surrounding the death, burial and resurrection of Jesus Christ! Do they make sure children know those things before they graduate? NO! In fact, to even mention His Name may just get you thrown out of school—and, you surely don't want to be seen studying His Word.

When I look at the fruit of their product, I tend to disregard the things that *they* say are important for a child to know. As homeschoolers, we have the opportunity, as well as the responsibility, to establish a balance in customizing and prioritizing the subjects and levels of knowledge required of our children in light of the outcome we hope to achieve.

It is sufficient for children to be made aware of certain facts by way of casual introduction (as opposed to indoctrination). By 'indoctrination' I mean grilling them, and quizzing them and testing them and retesting them and going over and over the material, etc. Anything beyond casual introduction detracts from eternal matters, confuses them as to their purpose on this earth.

Now, don't get the idea that I'm opposed to any kind of book-based education. Anyone who has visited us at Wisdom's Gate can tell you that we maintain a huge (and growing!) library. In fact, when folks come to our house they think they've accidentally wandered in to Books-R-Us! I doubt there's a room in our house where you cannot find a book! Rain or shine, if there's a used book swap or public library clearance we'll be there, down on our knees, rooting through boxes under tables like a chicken scratching for his first worm of the morning! Every one of my children are avid readers, but in everything we do (and read) we endeavor to seek first the Kingdom of our God knowing that all these other things will be added—in the Lord's timing—when we are ready for them and need them. Frankly, much of that is stuff they'll *never* need! So, why take up their brain space with it? Learn to see those little brains as a hard drive on a computer—you've only got so much space so go ahead and get your operating program (God's Will) and software (God's Word) installed first. They'll be much better equipped to handle all types of information and applications later.

To what are we training our children? If you do much gardening you know that you can train a vine. We all know that we're supposed to train up our children but some of us need to give a good bit more thought about what we are training them toward!! I've got no problem with the concept of raising children to be good citizens—as long as they're citizens of the right Kingdom. We are talking about two different kingdoms here. We are not in the same camp as the unGodly. As we saw earlier, we don't have the same goals. The issue is not just that some folks homeschool while others use the so-called public schools. It's that some folks serve their God with all their heart and all their mind—and some folks are keeping one foot angled back toward Egypt just in case they want to jump back over the fence!

The goal in Christian education is not merely to be *informed*, but to be *transformed* and *conformed* to His image. Make sure that your children are wholeheartedly applying themselves to learning those things that really matter and are of use to them in fulfilling God's plan for them, either now or in the future.

Now, that doesn't mean they should just sit around reading their Bibles all day long. For example, even younger children can participate in meal planning, grocery shopping, bread baking and food preservation which employ math and deductive skills with scientific applications, while teaching responsibility, stewardship and servanthood.

Learning such practically applicable skills as making their own soaps, shampoo, lotions and household cleaning supplies develops marketable skills, saves money, and increases knowledge of scientific formulas and applications.

In warm weather, besides being productive and mentally refreshing, planting flowers, doing yard work or tending gardens can be a highly educational time for the children (and for you). As a family, you'll learn botany, biology, ecology (all those things that went right over your head when you were in the government schools, right?) and all the while you'll be getting fresh air and sunshine and lots of physical exercise.

Homeschooling our children for the glory of God is a most exciting and rewarding endeavor—boredom simply has no place in a properly ordered homeschool setting. If you will acknowledge your need for the Lord's guidance in this area, He will certainly be faithful to direct your paths and show you how to establish your homeschool in a way that will bring life and joy to your children every day.

Whether academically or spiritually, you will know what each child needs at every juncture of their development. For instance, every child is different, are they not? Even identical twins can have opposite personalities.

...Some children fear displeasing their parents or disappointing their siblings or extended family members and, for this child, a simple word of instruction is usually enough.

...Some children are extremely selfish by nature, and are only willing to change course if the consequences of their actions will affect them directly and negatively. Some folks learn by reading, some folks learn by instruction, and some folks just have to touch the electric fence for themselves.

...Some have a moldable spirit and a genuine desire to do right but have not been consistently or properly trained.

We all are familiar with the blatantly rebellious child. He or she is generally uncooperative openly refusing to do right, angry, stomping around, moody, and a notorious door slammer. These in-your-face rebels will stop at nothing to get their way.

But, what about the child who lives a life of passive rebellion? This generally quiet child does not like to be told what to do, so he does it without being told in order to maintain a sense of control. He is outwardly conforming, but not truly with you in heart. This type of child can be extremely devious. Typically, this child is a model child in front of parents—a real, "Yes, Ma'am" kind of kid; always careful to avoid trouble at home. It is this type of child that you hear about on the news as having been found guilty of a heinous crime, while the neighbors all stand around and shake their heads saying, "But he was such a nice, quiet boy. Who would have ever imagined?"

Gary was a young man who was extremely gifted in many areas. Every year, he finished at the top of his class. Everything he attempted came easily to him. Everyone seemed to like him.

However, there was a flip side to his personality: He had a regular habit of sneaking out the window at night to go horsing around with his friends. One night in particular, things didn't go quite as smooth as planned and young Gary found himself racing home in a sweat with police hot on his heels. Quick as a flash he was in the window and under his covers trying his best to quiet his pounding heart and work up a hearty snore!

Not to be outdone by the young hooligan's shenanigans the policeman walked boldly up to the door and knocked loudly enough to wake up the parents sleeping inside (as well as the neighbors across the road).

"Ma'am, do you know where your son has been?"

"Why he's been sound asleep in his bed all evening."

"You're sure about that? Why don't you go check on him?"

Feigning grogginess and confusion, Gary climbed out of bed and proceeded to assure the officer amidst exaggerated yawns (as the parents stood by) that he surely must be mistaken.

Realizing that the parents were completely fooled by this slick performance, the officer could only issue a warning to the young man, "Well, I'm glad you are here where you belong. You'd better not let me catch you and your buddies out causing mischief or you'll be in big trouble!"

In total denial, the duped Mother exclaimed to her wayward son on the way back to bed, "Wasn't that sweet of that nice policeman to stop to make sure you were safe and sound?!"

Little did she know that her son's antics that evening could easily have cost him and his friends their very lives. It takes strong discernment in the Spirit to parent the passive rebellious child.

Then, there's the complancent/compliant child: this child is every parent's dream—right? Actually, this child would be classified as extremely high risk. Especially in large families where the parents may be dealing with one or more blatantly rebellious siblings, children in this category are the easiest to lose.

Why is this so? In a different setting, the same traits that make them seemingly model children (desire to "fit in," get along and not make waves, willingness to follow and do what they are told) can easily make them gang members.

How many times have you heard tragic stories of sin or violent crimes committed by a son who has gone wrong while his heartbroken mother sobs, "But he was such a good boy..."?

An effective, faithful parent who *truly knows* their child, will not justly bear the shame of a child's rebellion or irresponsibility on their watch. To nip rebellion in the bud in your household you must...

Face the truth! Our God has told us that, *"Foolishness is bound in the heart of a child"* (Proverbs 22:15). Like it or not, you must admit it—your child is no exception.

Listen! Ask questions. Draw the child out. Make time for them alone. Build a solid relationship with the child so that they will come to you when they are tempted or slipping in a certain area, confident of your love for them.

Observe! Manners, posture, gestures, verbal and facial expressions. The Biblical litmus test of Godly character is manifested in a child that is open to learn, eager to be taught, and hungry for the Word (Acts 17:11). That is exactly the type of open-heartedness your child must show toward your instruction.

Deal with the real issues! Are you longing for peace in your home? Arguments are never won. If you are facing a child who is questioning your authority, arguing back at you when you attempt to instruct or direct them, the real issue is not the surface conflict of the moment. If you fall into arguing over supposed areas of disagreement you will simply be digging the pit deeper. When these situations arise, the real problem is a refusal on the part of the child to recognize and accept his or her place under your authority. When this is dealt with appropriately, conflict is eliminated. There should be no discussion of peripheral issues until this is brought in line with God's Word. If a child is unsettled regarding that one issue, then *everything will be an issue!*

Test them! *"But He knoweth the way that I take: when He hath tried me, I shall come forth as gold"* (Job 23:10). Our God does not assume we are walking in obedience, He *knows*. Good or bad. We test our children academically, why not morally? This is not a gestapo approach to parenting, but rather, Biblical, loving, Godly parenting. *"As a father has compassion on his children, so the LORD has compassion on those who fear Him; for He knows how we are formed, He remembers that we are dust"* (Psalm 103:13,14).

Obey God! Follow the Scriptures religiously! Stay within the guidelines! God has warned us in advance of the pitfalls of certain patterns and activities. Do not make the mistake of thinking that you can ignore those warnings without certain disaster. For example: *"Be not deceived: evil communications* [bad companions] *corrupt good manners"* (1 Corinthians 15:33). Don't kid yourself. This also applies to music, movies, TV, and all social contacts.

"Follow peace with all men, and holiness, without which no man shall see the Lord" (Hebrews 12:14). If we fail to train our children toward holy living, we've not only failed them in this life as we saw earlier, we've failed them for eternity.

WHAT ARE THE LORD'S REQUIREMENTS?

"He hath shewed thee, O man, what is good; and what doth the LORD require of thee, but to do justly [honesty, integrity, faithfulness, trustworthiness, dependability vs. lying, unfairness]*, and to love mercy* [generosity, compassion, forgiveness vs. greed, selfishness, bullying, uncaring]*, and to walk humbly* [humility, peaceable, esteeming others vs. pride, arrogance, haughtiness, anger, self-absorbed] *with thy God"* (Micah 6:8).

These are the things for which the Lord will hold us accountable. To truly understand the requirements of our God, we must truly know Him through obedience to His Word by the power of His Holy Spirit. It is in this way that we can, with authority, introduce Him to our children and train them as disciples for His Kingdom. There is no higher calling than this!

WHEN REBELLION HITS HOME

"For the son dishonoureth the father, the daughter riseth up against her mother, the daughter in law against her mother in law; a man's enemies are the men of his own house. Therefore I will look unto the LORD; I will wait for the God of my salvation: my God will hear me" (Micah 7:6,7).

Is your home life filled with the sweet sounds of laughter, happy singing, and love? Is that your heart's desire? Know this for certain; you do not have to endure discord and strife as an inevitable part of your daily life.

In order to achieve the peace and harmony that is characteristic of a Godly home, you must understand that early detection of unGodly character flaws coupled with a clear understanding of God's high and holy standards is the prerequisite to reaching that goal.

The medical industry has long recognized the value of "early detection" in treating potentially fatal diseases. They understand that once a cancer has taken hold, it is often impossible to eradicate it from the body. In fact, once the immune system has been broken down and disarmed by the long-term presence of the degenerative disease, the body's natural defenses will often "defend" the killer's right to be there against all attempts to rescue the body and bring it back to health.

If we continually resist the attempts of the Holy Spirit to speak to our heart and prick our conscience, we will eventually become confused in our thinking and vulnerable to the attacks of the enemy of our souls.

If a child will not open his heart to instruction and correction, his life will be out of tune with God's plan and is surely headed for pain and destruction. He will be as unfitting in the family circle as a sour note jangling amidst the lovely sounds emanating from the perfectly prepared score of God's beautiful and eternal concert of life.

When it comes to preventative maintenance when dealing with a rebel, we can learn much from Adam and Eve (the first recorded example of Biblical parenting). The fourth chapter of Genesis tells us the story of two brothers—both raised by the same parents, and yet, with a completely different outcome.

One flag that I see in this account is that, when trouble started brewing, the parents were seemingly not around—or, at least, were apparently in oblivion to the fact that their son was not in a good place. Cain's full-blown state of rebellion is evident in the fact that he had no genuine love for anyone else but was a self-willed, argumentative (vs. 8), angry (vs. 5) young man who was totally absorbed in himself (vs. 9,13,14). These first parents may never have won the heart of Cain no matter how hard they may have tried (remember, Cain slew Abel *after* God, Himself, sat him down and tried to set him straight; vs. 6,7), but had their parenting style been a faithful mirror of the Father's heart (vs. 5-7), once his rebellion became obvious, they would have dealt with him only under the conditions that God had established in His own communication with Cain (vs. 5,7). They would have isolated him from his siblings once it became apparent that he was having an attitude problem and was unwilling to live by the rules (vs. 3-5) and would have accepted him back into their good graces only when he was ready and willing to respond properly. In doing so, they probably would not have lost Abel. As it was, they ended up losing both sons.

Rebellion is not just a phase that a child is going through. It is a grievous SIN that has dire consequences and a potentially far-reaching negative impact.

"*And Samuel said, Hath the LORD as great delight in burnt offerings and sacrifices, as in obeying the voice of the LORD? Behold, to obey is better than sacrifice, and to hearken than the fat of rams. For rebellion is as the sin of witchcraft, and stubbornness is as iniquity and idolatry. Because thou hast rejected the word of the LORD, He hath also rejected thee from being king*" (1 Samuel 15: 22,23).

Our children will never learn that sin has consequences if we are not faithful to carry through and allow those consequences to come to pass once our counsel and authority has been rejected.

It is an undisputed fact that our God is a God of love (John 3:16,17). Yet, while God's *love* can be construed as unconditional

(Romans 5:8), the *requirements for relationship with Him* are certainly not unconditional. For instance, it is not His will that any should perish, but that all should come to repentance (2 Peter 3:9) but the terms to appropriating such mercy and qualifying as recipients of that blessing have been clearly spelled out in the Scriptures—and they are *very* conditional.

Godly parenting will always clearly reflect and accurately portray the heart and mind of God our Heavenly Father. Trying to be "nicer than Jesus" in our parenting style will only result in disaster.

In the case of the prodigal son (Luke 15:11-32), our God has given us a classic example of tough parental love in action. Because the rebellious son was allowed to reap the consequences of the riotous living he stubbornly chose to sow, he came to feel the pain of his own choices and to understand that his actions were sinful. He had been taught well under his father's roof and knew exactly what was expected of him there. Therefore, he eventually saw that he needed to accept full responsibility for his actions and repent.

Had his father been weak and made concessions to him in his rebellion—had he been allowed to come home whenever he liked, to sit at his father's table and partake of the good fruits of that home, to hit Dad up for more money and resources whenever he had squandered the wealth which had been made available to him—he likely would never have understood his desperate spiritual condition or been able to find a clearly-defined way back home.

Obviously, the father loved his son as is evident by his joyous response to his repentant son's humble return but, prior to that happy day, he faithfully displayed a Godly form of love that has the capacity to be both tough and tender at the same time. He did not go chasing after his son, threatening, begging and pleading with him to return. He remained faithful in his place at home and, overcoming his fears despite the bleak circumstances, trusted God with an active faith for the outcome—and God abundantly rewarded his faith!

THE IMPORTANCE OF EARLY TRAINING

It is interesting to note that, while pagan systems of philosophy do not acknowledge the existence of our God, they operate under a Biblical principle in recognizing that, in order for their anti-Christ goals and agenda to succeed, early access to the child is imperative.

As Christian homeschooling parents, we all know and believe the truth of the Scriptural commandment to "train up a child in the way he should go," knowing that following that command is the promise, "and when he is old, he will not depart from it."

Consider the alternative and ask yourself this question: if we *fail* to train up the child in the way he should go, will we be able to successfully steer him in another direction when he is old? You've heard the saying, "Old habits die hard." Think about it…

If a child has been allowed to go his own way and, thereby, has been *trained* toward unruliness, or if a child has had his every whim catered to and, thereby, has been *trained* toward self-indulgence, or if a child has not been taught discipline and the value of hard work and, thereby, has been *trained* toward laziness, or if a child has not been taught self-control and, thereby, has been *trained* toward unrestrained emotional outbursts of anger and frustration, then the child will battle these character weaknesses in every area of his life throughout his time on this earth.

PARENTING THAT REFLECTS THE FATHER'S LOVE

"Though I speak with the tongues of men and of angels, and have not charity [love], *I am become as sounding brass, or a tinkling cymbal"* (1 Corinthians 13:1).

Love—without it, everything has an unpleasant or hollow ring to it. It is love that motivates us to raise our children for the glory of our God. Not only is it true that love covers a multitude of sins, it also prevents sin! A heart full of love for others will not allow a person to sin against God or others.

Successful homeschooling requires that a perfect and holy love must first be rooted and manifest in the hearts and lives of the parent. It is no accident that the best adult education program available today is most effectively achieved in a home filled with infants, toddlers, children and teenagers. Homeschooling is as much about parents being discipled by the Heavenly Father, as it is about children being discipled by their parents. You simply cannot teach the harmonies of a song that you do not know.

Our God is certainly in the business of turning the hearts of the fathers (parents) toward their children (Malachi 4:6). The more you come to know the Lord, the more you will understand yourself—and your children! Each and every one of them! There is no patent formula—no "one-size-fits-all" methodology for child training. Every child is different, are they not? Even identical twins can have opposite personalities.

Maybe you think it's already too late to effectively train your children. What makes you think so? Don't give in to the devil's lies! Has God told you that? Have you been lax (or possibly over-zealous) in your responsibility as a parent? If you've not been faithful to parent your children according to Biblical principles, then *repent* and start *now* to train your sons and daughters. Whether you are raising toddlers or teens, consistent Biblical discipline and Godly instruction should have them singing a new tune in no time!

FEARLESS PARENTING

Some parents feel inadequate for the job of parenting or overwhelmed by the responsibility it carries. Others fear they will lose their children's love if they insist on upholding and requiring a high moral standard.

To quote the angel who appeared to announce to the mother of Jesus that she was going to be a parent—"FEAR NOT!" Fear will only bring about that which you fear most. Faith is the key that will keep the paralyzing effects of fear far from you.

Parents often come to me saying, "Homeschooling is so hard. I just don't think I can do this." Listen! That very statement is laden with accusation against your God. The truth of the matter is that, in giving you children, God has *not* given you more than you can bear. Stop whimpering and whining—stand up and face the responsibility before you as a parent with courage and dignity. There is absolutely no way that you can afford *not* to actively and faithfully teach and train your own children. To do so, will bring glory to our God. To fail to do so will only bring misery to your household as well as bring a reproach on the Name of our Lord. However, if you have done your best before the Lord to train up your child according to Biblical principles, and he willfully rejects your place in his life, the responsibility and burden of his sin will not rest upon your shoulders. *"He that wasteth his father, and chaseth away his mother, is a son that causeth shame, and bringeth reproach"* (Proverbs 19:26).

Don't be bullied into a passive parental stance by the purveyors of the myth of unconditional love that has no requirements to relationship. Our God expressed a very conditional kind of love when He said, *"I love them that love Me..."* (Proverbs 8:17). There's nothing wrong with setting a standard that says, "If you want to be part of this family, you must walk in love and abide by the rules." That standard is a faithful portrayal of the love of the Heavenly Father as expressed by Jesus:

"If ye keep My commandments, ye shall abide in My love" (John 15:10).

Jesus clearly set the standard for good standing in family relationships when he established his criteria for evaluating those relationships. *"There was a crowd around Jesus, and someone said, 'Your mother and Your brothers and sisters are outside, asking for You.' Jesus replied, 'Who is My mother? Who are My brothers?' Then He looked at those around Him and said, 'These are My mother and brothers. Anyone who does God's will is My brother and sister and mother'"* (Mark 3:32-35).

THE HEART OF A REBEL

It is so easy for those, whose children have done well, to pass heavy judgment on families who are facing rebellion in one or more of their children. However, most parents of rebellious or wayward children beat themselves up plenty ("Should I have done such-and-such?" and "If only I would not have done this-or-that!") and we should exercise extreme caution so as not to be guilty of heaping illegitimate guilt on an already grieving Brother or Sister who, if dealing with a prodigal who has fully given themselves over to their rebellion, is already suffering beyond what those who have never walked that road can even begin to imagine. Everyone's situation is different and we must be very careful that we only speak what truly reflects the whole heart, mind and counsel of our God about any particular set of circumstances.

The fact is, some obstinate older children just rebel at the first opportunity that presents itself simply because they finally can. The child's outwardly obedient lifestyle while growing up was never born out of Spirit-led conviction despite the parents' best efforts and through no genuine fault or failure on their part. This circumstance is a reflection of the child's character and not necessarily that of the parent/teacher.

Jesus was the finest teacher to ever walk the planet. The rich, young ruler went away sad not because Jesus had failed to explain things to him properly or in a nice manner, but because he wasn't willing to pay the price required of him. (Matthew 19:16-22) Yet, Jesus didn't run after him and renegotiate the deal in order to "preserve the relationship." Judas had all the same training as the other disciples yet turned out to be a bad egg. So, can we really conclude that Jesus blew it because Judas had his own ideas about how things ought to be?

As long as there is free-will (i.e., as long as we live on this side of the Pearly Gates) there will be rebels in our midst. A rebel is one who, having heard and understood the requirements for righteousness has rejected the truth and turned aside to go his/her own way. A rebel will resent any attempts to place controls on his or her life, but the heart of a true son or daughter will recognize and respond to loving parenting, and will eventually come to know and accept his or her place under the parents' God-ordained authority. A Godly parent who has done everything humanly possible to get through to a stiff-necked rebel without success need not allow the enemy of our souls to heap false condemnation on top of their boundless grief. If the unvarnished results of a thorough search of our heart do not condemn us, neither does He. Be comforted in His love and His understanding of what you are suffering. Place the child firmly in His capable hands and allow Him to work all things for the good of all involved.

God is not an unreasonable task-master Who requires a standard beyond what you are capable of delivering. He Who made us knows that we are but dust. Try as you may, you will never be the perfect parent—still you must try and give it your wholehearted effort. Remember that He Who walked in absolute perfection on this earth was rejected by the very ones who sat under His teaching daily and were closest to Him. He knows full well just what we are facing in trying to bring His light into this dark world. He is fully aware that each of your children has a mind and will of his/her own. Don't carry an illegitimate burden of guilt or responsibility beyond what our God will require of you. Just do your prayerful best and He'll take care of the rest.

"For as the heaven is high above the earth, so great is His mercy toward them that fear Him. As far as the east is from the west, so far hath He removed our transgressions from us. Like as a father pitieth His children, so the LORD pitieth them that fear Him. For He knoweth our frame; He remembereth that we are dust. As for man, his days are as grass: as a flower of the field, so he flourisheth. For the wind passeth over it, and it is gone; and the place thereof shall know it no more. But the mercy of the LORD is from everlasting to everlasting upon them that fear Him, and His righteousness unto children's children, to such as keep His covenant, and to those that remember His commandments to do them" (Psalm 103 11-17).

Parenting With Jesus

LEARNING FROM JESUS

As a parent, I see many parallels in Jesus thoughts and life compared to our own experience. Though He never married or raised earthly children in this life, He is still our prime example for all things pertaining to parenting and a Godly family life.

"Take My yoke upon you, and learn of Me; for I am meek and lowly in heart" (Matthew 11:29).

One of the first things we can learn from Jesus is His meekness. A father or mother who are prone to skulking around the house, roaring about this and that, ready to pounce on the least little thing, is not going to conjure up desirable images of our meek and humble Lord Jesus in the minds of the children in that household (1 Peter 5:8).

It is a known fact that our children are far more influenced by what we *do* than by what we profess. They are looking and listening for the truth—and the human tendency is to believe our eyes before our ears!

Jesus has told us that, *"I am the vine, ye are the branches: He that abideth in Me, and I in him, the same bringeth forth much fruit: for without Me ye can do nothing"* (John 15:5). Let's face it—parenting is not a job for sissies! Don't try it without Jesus.

FOLLOWING JESUS

It is only insomuch as we, ourselves, are closely following Jesus, that we will be able to lead our children along a right path.

The story is told of a young lad who lived years ago in the city of Chicago. His father had a habit of sleeping late, getting up quietly, and sneaking out of the house to head back down to the bar where he would proceed to drink the night away before staggering back home long after the children had fallen asleep. One winter day, as the father slowly made his way through several feet of freshly-fallen snow, from somewhere not far behind him, he heard the faint call of his young son, "Daddy, look! I'm walking in your steps! I'm following in your steps, Daddy! Look! I'm walking just like you!" Turning around he saw the little fellow stepping with big striding steps directly into each footprint he had just made. With horror, the thought struck him that in just a few more steps, he would be leading his innocent little son right into that sin-filled bar to which he was headed! Instantly, the father turned to face the child and dropping to his knees in the snow, cried out, "Lord Jesus! If my son is going to follow so closely in my footsteps then, with Your strength and by Your grace, I will follow Your lead in a more righteous direction!"

The first step toward a parenting style that will reflect the pure and holy image of Jesus is that of humility and a teachable spirit. If we are honest with ourselves we wouldn't want our children to follow in *our* footsteps and do many of the things that we have done. *What we really want is for them to follow Jesus.*

REFLECTING JESUS

"Jesus saith unto him, I am the Way, the Truth, and the Life: no man cometh unto the Father, but by Me. If ye had known Me, ye should have known My Father also: and from henceforth ye know Him, and have seen Him" (John 14:6-7).

It is not enough for us, as parents, to merely teach our children facts *about* Jesus. We need to introduce our children, personally, to Him. Even more importantly, we must reflect the image of the Father so that when they look at us, they will see Him, and recognize Him, and learn to heed His voice.

Just the fact that, by God's design, they will spend the greatest share of their most formative years with their parents should make us realize that the burden of their eternal souls rests with us. It is parents, over anyone else on this earth who, in their children's formative years, bear the weight and shoulder the responsibility of leading them to Christ.

A careful and thorough study of the life of Jesus will provide great insight into just how we may actively, practically, and effectively "show them the Father."

"And whatsoever ye shall ask in My name, that will I do, that the Father may be glorified in the Son. If ye shall ask any thing in My name, I will do it" (John 14:13-14).

Parents who would mirror the heart of the Father must demonstrate an eagerness to provide for the needs of their children without grudging. Children should feel totally at liberty to bring to their parents any needs, desires, fears—anything at all—fully confident of obtaining a compassionate hearing.

Does this mean that we are to be human vending machines ready to dish out all manner of goodies in response to whatever buttons the child is pushing to satisfy his every whim? Absolutely not! Parents who attempt to operate a 24-hour, seven days a week, catering service to accommodate the unbridled and selfish natures of their children will soon find themselves disillusioned with the job and headed for a lifetime of disappointment.

OBEYING JESUS

Not only does love constrain us to *give* to our families beyond our self-centered human tendencies, it also constrains us to *require* something of them. True parental love, which reflects the heart of the Heavenly Father, demands obedience.

"If ye love Me, keep My commandments" (John 14:15). *"This is My commandment, That ye love one another, as I have loved you. Greater love hath no man than this, that a man lay down his life for his friends. Ye are My friends, if ye do whatsoever I command you"* (John 15:12-14).

Obedience and sacrifice are inextricably intertwined throughout Scripture. Homeschooling is a sacrifice. We willingly make that sacrifice for our children out of a heart's desire to walk in obedience to His will. As our children witness our faithfulness in denying ourselves, taking up our cross daily, and following Jesus in the way He has shown us to go as parents, they will begin to know and understand the heart of the Father. When our children learn that Jesus laid down His life for us, they will know that it is that same Jesus in us Who gives us the grace to serve the Lord and others, and to live each day for something beyond ourselves.

"Philip saith unto Him, 'Lord, shew us the Father, and it sufficeth us'" (John 14:8).

Most children love to hear their parents read Bible stories aloud to them, but as children grow older, the deepest longing of their hearts is to *see* Jesus—sitting at their table or on their bed, listening to them share what is on their hearts, speaking words of comfort and encouragement (and even bringing instruction and direction) at just the right time.

Jesus didn't fret over whether or not His disciples had completed their Math and Science lessons, or passed the SAT, or obtained their GED. Jesus didn't get stressed out about soaring food prices, the stock market, or world events. He did not get so wrapped up in His job that He forgot about the things that mattered the most. He kept His priorities in order by doing only that which the Father told Him to do, and displayed His total trust in the Father by walking through this life shrouded in a peace that passed all understanding. *Nothing* rocked His boat—literally.

BRINGING JESUS TO THE WORLD

People were willing to walk for miles along dusty roads over rough terrain, to sit all day in the hot sun, without food or basic comforts, just to see Jesus and hear what He had to say.

Folks are not that much different now than they were in Jesus' day. The masses of people (our children included) are still longing to get even just the slightest glimpse of Jesus. They are still desperate for just one touch from the Master Healer. They would still give up food and the comforts of home to hear a life-giving message that contains the clear ring of truth that can only come from Him.

What folks have grown tired of nowadays is a watered-down gospel that holds to a form of Godliness while denying the power thereof. They've grown tired of modern-day Pharisees and religious bigots and hypocrites. They've grown tired of dead churches and worldly substitutes for genuine Christianity. They've grown tired of vain ritual and endless activities and programs, and hype and rhetoric and sham.

What we all need—what we all truly long for—is to see Jesus. Why not hide yourself in the Rock of Ages and let your children see Jesus living in you today?

"LORD, shew us the Father, and it sufficeth us" (John 14:8).

Ways We Make it Hard on Ourselves

Most people begin homeschooling with high hopes and the best of intentions mingled, invariably, with a reasonable degree of apprehension and trepidation. It takes an uncommon courage to make the necessary sacrifices to take such a step.

However, homeschooling, itself, does not guarantee you a positive outcome. After 30 years of involvement in the homeschool movement, I've seen (and you probably have also) too many parents who have homeschooled and ended up losing their children to the world anyway. So, if you're thinking of homeschooling as the end-all, beat-all, cure-all, fix-all, I can tell you right up front—it's not.

Your particular view of homeschooling will greatly affect the ultimate results. A truly Biblical approach to learning will carry you a long way towards real and lasting success. It will also ensure that we do not raise career-driven, workaholics who become overwhelmed with the burdens of this life! God-directed homeschooling will never leave you feeling the effects of overload syndrome.

Let me show you what I mean. Take automobiles, for instance. Automobiles are helpful vehicles. Yet, I found out the hard way that if you treat your little family car like a paper delivery truck and overload it by trying to haul thousands of magazines, you are likely to experience a breakdown. Washing machines and clothes dryers can be great tools for lightening a busy mother's workload. However, if you overload the washer or dryer the effect is counter-productive. You'll end up with a damp, wrinkled, dirty mess. You need to break those loads down into manageable proportions if you are going to be pleased with the outcome. Food is another commodity that was part of God's plan for sustaining life. Hey, it's a good thing! But, too much of a good thing is not a good thing! If we overload our digestive systems, regardless of how healthy our food choices, we are going to be in misery for a while.

It somewhat reminds me of the plan my girls came up with years ago. Someone provided us with a boatload of "yummy" children's chewable vitamins, which I dutifully instructed the girls to ingest on a daily basis. However, if the choking, gagging, moaning, retching sounds accompanied by shudders and horrible faces were any indication, none of the girls liked taking them—except for Bethany Rose who didn't seem to mind the taste one bit.

Day after day the girls obediently persisted in being good stewards of this bountiful provision, all the while reminding themselves of the far greater sufferings of other martyrs who had already gone on to their rewards. However, such comforting thoughts as, "At least it's not as bad as being burned at the stake!" ultimately began to lose their motivational impact.

Finally, they came up with an ingenious solution. After much cajoling on the part of her sisters (and completely without my knowledge), Bethany finally agreed to "volunteer" to become a surrogate vitamin taker and swallow each of her sister's vitamins in proxy. While this seemed like the charitable thing to do in order to prevent further "agony" for her sisters, not only did this solution really not do them any good, in reality, it soon became undeniably apparent to all concerned that such imbalance was not healthy for Bethany, either.

As we have noted, Christian homeschooling could be more specifically defined as Biblically-based education that produces Godly character and prepares the student for a lifetime of faithful service to God. Homeschooling that brings Glory to God is God-inspired, God-motivated, God-driven, God-directed, and God-blessed. The secret to successfully managing your homeschool is to keep your priorities in order. The ultimate goal should be to meet God's requirements for homeschooling—and not someone else's.

Overloading is one of the main factors that contribute to the malady known as "homeschool burnout." When the homeschool load begins to feel HEAVY, mark my words, you've taken on more than the Lord intended. Somewhere along the way, we have picked up something that our God never intended for us to carry. *"Take My yoke upon you and learn from Me, for I am gentle and humble in heart, and you will find rest for your souls. For My yoke is easy and My burden is light"* (Matt. 11:29, 30).

One of the most common overloading mistakes that homeschoolers make is...

ACADEMIC OVERLOAD

Many parents lack clearly defined goals for their homeschool and are far too laid back in their child-training methodology. At the other extreme, there is often a tendency among some parents to push young children to learn before they are developmentally ready. Maybe it's to impress the neighbors or to prove to the grandparents that the children really are learning, but the motivation for this approach is born out of fear or pride—and never of the Spirit. In later years, this same tendency will manifest itself in the parent by trying to cover far too many subjects, at levels too high to be reasonably attained, in an unreasonably short period of time.

We've all heard of parents pushing their children so that they can be the youngest person to enter Harvard, or Yale, or even the local community college. Spiritual and emotional problems (such as depression) are very common in these young people who have been the innocent victims of their parents' unrestrained egotism. Something dies in the heart of a child who has been pushed to attain a specific, academic goal without an eternal perspective in view.

Don't misunderstand. I am not against focused early childhood education. By the time my babies were two years old, I was teaching them how to read. What I am against is worldly indoctrination with non-essential information during the most formative years of their lives. Instead of cramming my children's heads with a textbook education which scope and sequence was based on the government's idea of what is important, we were learning about our God and His Kingdom and this world that He has created and how we fit in to His plans in the larger scheme of things.

If you've ever been to a homeschool curriculum fair or convention, you know that, when it comes to educational resources, we have an abundance of options and they do not come in a one-size-fits-all package. Learning styles and preferences are as varied as the wide array of curricula and it is crucial that you search prayerfully through all those captivating options. The possibilities for learning are endless and there is no sense getting bogged down in a program (no matter how many stars, or hearts, or thumbs up it got from some product reviewer) that just doesn't fit your needs.

To fulfill God's purposes, academic goals must always be Biblically defined and supported, and Spiritually inspired. Teaching children to count is not as important as teaching them what counts! You may be their primary teacher but (like it or not) they are going to pick up all kinds of things along the way that they did not necessarily learn from you.

I'm not at all suggesting that all you have to do is just throw your children out in the back yard and one day they'll come running in with their Ph.D.! Homeschooling is a building process and having the right foundation is what will ultimately insure the structural integrity of your finished product.

You'll never get to the place in homeschooling known as having "arrived." You'll never be spending your days cruising on easy street. If you think you're cruising through this process, you'd better get with God because it's not so much that you've arrived—it's just that it's all going right over your head!!! There are definitely some things you need Him to help you see.

Whenever we are dealing with a problem we must get to the root. An examination of the root of academic overload reveals an underlying problem—expectation overload.

So many homeschooling parents have fallen into the trap of having unrealistic expectations. Where do these come from? Unrealistic expectations are based on worldly standards, so that the child's self-concept is built around whether he measures up and when. This can be utterly devastating to a child. It causes him to lose all sense of his real value and place in this world.

Think about it ... what is the first thing a stranger will say to your child? "Where do you go to school? What grade are you in?" That is the standard by which folks want to measure your child. Where do they get that? Show me the chapter and verse from the Scriptures! According to Biblical standards, you're just not going to find justification for that kind of departmentalization.

Pushing children to achieve the highest score, or to graduate ahead of other children their age, or be the youngest person to be accepted into any school is not only unwise—it is a sin. Why? As Christians, we cannot embrace or enforce an extra-Biblical standard. To do so is to require a standard that our God does not require. To arbitrarily follow and embrace the worldly and carnal man's philosophy of education is not a goal that can be pursued in full confidence and faith that it is pleasing to the Lord or in compliance with His will—and He says that whatever is not of faith is sin.

So, we need to ask ourselves this question: who are you allowing to set the goals and standards for your homeschool?

The government? When you first started looking into this experience we call homeschooling, and trying to figure out, "How am I going to go about this?" where did you go for information? Did you go online or to the library to get a copy of the State requirement? Is the government setting the goals and standards for your homeschool?

Is it your mother-in-law? Or that relative or neighbor who also just happens to have a teaching degree and holds a position as a teacher down at the local government school?

Or, maybe it's your homeschool support group? Are you looking to them for guidance and direction, or legal coverage as an umbrella to shelter under, or their opinion of *what* needs to be taught ... *when* it needs to be taught ... *how* it needs to be taught?

Or, is it your God?

When you start feeling overwhelmed, remind yourself that God's requirements are so simple: He only asks that we live justly, love mercy, and walk humbly with Him.

What a relief! Every once in a while I just kind of pull back and I say to myself, "Really, now! Homeschooling is not hard at all!"

Maximizing Your Efficiency

God sets the solitary in families for a reason (Psalm 68:6). Every member of the family should bear a measure of responsibility appropriate to their age or ability. When the load becomes imbalanced, it will surely result in a responsibility overload that is sure to topple even the most willing servant.

For the child, this can mean requiring the child to make adult decisions that he is not capable of making, or for which he should not shoulder the burden and responsibility.

For example, have you ever observed a parent asking a toddler to express preferences such as which balloon he wants—the red one or the blue one? Or, asking a young child which clothes he wants to wear or whether he wants eggs or cereal for breakfast? (Frankly, this was never a problem at our house because we were so poor when the children were little that they really never had more than two choices at any given meal—take it or leave it!)

Early exposure to unlimited choices will engender selfishness and ingratitude ("but, I wanted a *blue* bike, not a *red* one!") rather than an appreciation for the basic provisions of the Lord. It can leave the child with the impression that all the world is just waiting for his will to be expressed or imposed.

A child's legitimate need is simply to know that there *is* food for him to eat and clothing for him to wear. To train him in the direction of his wants and desires (beyond genuine need) is to feed and cultivate his carnal nature and to nurture a willful spirit that will ultimately hinder him later in life.

Young children have a deep need to feel covered and cared-for—not independent and self-sufficient. There will be plenty of time, when they are older, for them to decide every manner of issues for the rest of their lives. For now, why not do the merciful thing and just allow them to be children?

In order to avoid responsibility overload in your children, make every effort to establish and enforce specific patterns, rules, and guidelines for your home and the members of your household. Set up a schedule. It can, and should, be flexible, but it should be resolutely in place and adhered to as much as possible, nonetheless.

Even if you have a child who seems self-confident and acts like he wishes independence, it is not in the child's best interest to give it to him. If you are faithful to provide a peaceful, quiet, ordered, secure, controlled atmosphere, once the child is confident of its consistency, he or she will come to rest in it. Children feel more secure when they know their boundaries and limits, and the guidelines and rules are consistently enforced.

The serenity that these simple principles will bring to your home is a lasting blessing that you can give to your child.

When folks ask, "How do you manage to do it all? I mean, you're a single parent, and you homeschool, and you have this publishing-speaking-writing ministry to keep up with—how do you ever manage to do it all?" I tell them the truth. I *can't* do it all—and, neither can you. The Bible tells us that apart from God, we can do nothing. To believe anything other than that is just arrogance.

So, what is the answer? One sure way for a homeschooling parent to effectively manage their homeschool and avoid responsibility overload is to demonstrate and delegate! Stop trying to do everything for everyone and, instead, start teaching and training them to do things for themselves.

Hopefully, you know how to do math (or at least how to run a calculator!) and read and write, and spell (or at least you know how to run the spell-checker on your computer). You know how to cook, clean, do laundry, keep the house in order, balance a checkbook, and countless other skills which you've acquired over the years. Children, obviously, are not born with this knowledge. Once your children reach a teachable age, your job description changes just a bit. Rather than continuing to single-handedly do all these things for your family—like you did when they were helpless babies—your job, at this stage, is to teach and train your children to do these things to the point that, eventually, they can do everything that you know how to do without your prompting or oversight. Before you know it, they'll be teaching you a thing or two!

Learn to perform mutually compatible tasks simultaneously. For example, you can easily fold a load of clothes while talking on the phone. Another multi-tasking opportunity that presents itself daily is the time spent washing and drying the dishes (or loading the dishwasher, as the case may be). While applying yourself to this mindless task, try coaching children on memorization of facts, or quizzing children on their work, or orally grading papers. This is a much better approach as children learn immediately not only that they gave the wrong answer, but they'll learn *why* the answer was wrong which is much less discouraging to a child.

We've all heard the health enthusiasts' rally cry, "No pain, no gain." While in many countries women walk several miles a day just to fetch and tote a day's provision of water for their families, here in America comfort and ease are the norm and the general philosophy is more along the lines of, "no pain, no pain."

In this day of modern conveniences, it is well worth the effort to look for ways to stretch yourself beyond your comfort zone. Rather than arranging your house with an eye toward ease and comfort, consider setting up your house so that you are getting good, natural exercise as you go about normal daily tasks.

Not only can we learn to make our work even more profitable by combining tasks (and, therefore, benefits) we can also make our daily routine more enjoyable.

Play inspirational or educational tapes or CDs while showering or taking a bath or while driving to and from appointments. (*Pilgrim's Progress* audio series is a family favorite that we've also carried in our product line for years.) Make sure that you're getting positive input to recharge your batteries on a daily basis.

Pray while hanging the laundry or driving your car (I would strongly suggest learning to pray with your eyes open for these activities—especially while driving!).

You may fellowship with family members, memorize Scripture, or sing together while doing the dishes. Make sure that, when you are interacting with your children you give them your undivided attention. I'll be honest with you—for me, that is a constant battle. Sometimes, my children would come in while I was working (usually while trying to do several things at once) and they'd be talking away to me before I realized that I hadn't even looked at them. I was just there staring intently at my work going, "UmHm. Yeah. UmHm. Okay..." and acting like I'd really heard them. Sometimes, I approved things that I never would have approved had I really been paying full attention! They'd just say, "Thanks, Mom!" and they'd run with it! If you're daydreaming nothing will wake you up faster than when your child goes skipping off hollering, "She said, YES!" while you're standing there asking yourself, "What did I say YES to?" I guarantee you, I'd quickly come to attention and go find out exactly what I said YES to and make sure I really *meant* YES!!

To this day I'm still learning to stop what I'm doing, turn toward them, look them in the eye and say, "I'm sorry. I was distracted here with all this stuff. Tell me again. What was it you said?" Speak their name. Let them know you're really with them. They appreciate that. Just that little bit of common courtesy says, "I care about you. You are my priority." You love them and they know it.

Team up with friends, family members or neighbors when it comes to big jobs such as gardening, canning, Once-A-Month Cooking, etc. If you are working together with Christians, this provides a welcome opportunity for fellowship and makes time pass quickly. If you are working with unbelievers, you'll have an excellent opportunity to shine your light as you work together.

Don't be too proud to ask for or receive help when necessary. Face the fact that you are naturally restricted by our common human limitations and content yourself to live within those normal boundaries that our God has established. Be satisfied to allow Him to get all the glory for everything you do in His Name. If you make it your ambition to do only what He has for you to do in any day's time, life will never become an unbearable burden and your efforts will not go unrewarded. As you faithfully homeschool your children for His glory, He will daily receive your sacrifice as a sweet-smelling offering of praise to Him. When all is said and done, it will have been worth all the effort!

Just Say No to Over-Commitment

The day that I had to move up to a daily scheduler that featured *two pages* to record each day's activities, it occurred to me that I just might (possibly) be facing a scheduling overload. Somehow, the majority of folks I know crossed over long ago into full-blown insanity when it comes to thinking they can do it all, have it all, be it all—and never have to pay the going rate.

Joining every extra class and attending every youth group function or field trip that's offered by your local support group is a common mistake that many homeschooling families make. Now, I'm not saying that those things are wrong or that we should never take the children on a field trip. It is just that it is difficult to maintain the standards and disciplines of the home when too much time is spent on the go in a public setting—and that includes time spent around other homeschooling families. After all, homeschooling is just that—HOMEschooling. We've run those two words together until they've taken on a meaning all their own. The key to true and lasting success in this context lies in recognizing the inherent value hidden in those first four letters—H-O-M-E. Proper training of children involves devoting undivided, uninterrupted, quality time to communicating and walking out those lessons that we must teach (and learn) on a line-upon-line, day-to-day basis. If over-commitment has become a pitfall to your homeschooling efforts, you need to turn around and establish HOME as your foundation and your base.

Let's consider for just a moment a common malady to which we all are susceptible if we are not extremely careful—over-commitment to church activities. These pursuits (especially the age-segregated variety) are notorious for depleting quality family time. Monday night choir practice, Tuesday night church board and deaconess meeting, Wednesday evening prayer meeting, Thursday's Mom's-Night-Out, Friday night youth group, Saturday morning men's prayer breakfast, and Sunday School and preaching services twice on Sunday do not leave much time for a peaceful, unified family. If one or more members of your family are absent from the home (or simply separated from each other) for non-essential reasons several times each week, regardless of the activity, consider re-examining your priorities and commitments.

Before I came to God, we were avid church-goers who did all that stuff, but after I came to know the God that we serve today, and to understand His will for our lives, we pulled out of most of those activities. When I first brought the children home, let me tell you—they were NOT happy campers!! I think today, with hindsight, they would tell you it was a blessing in disguise but, in the beginning, I'll guarantee you, they were not rising up and calling me blessed!!

Now, that's not to say that we never went anywhere or never did anything, but we started to focus on *doing things together* as a family. We purposefully avoided any activity where as soon as you came through the door, somebody stepped up and said, "Oh, you're ten. You go downstairs. Mom, you can go in there with the ladies but that little one has to go to the nursery."

Remember that old saying, "the family that prays together, stays together"? Well, in this day and age, it seems the more logical argument would be that "the family that *stays* together, prays together." It's downright difficult, if not impossible, to establish a pattern of praying together as a family when you are not physically together most of the time. Even then, it can be a challenge.

When you are together day in and day out—inevitably, at times, somewhat rubbing each other the wrong way—you also have the blessing of being able to pray together over those very things. You are able to cement those relationships and experience a bonding. Then there are those times when that child who, earlier in the day had that *look* (even though they are smart enough not to speak it outright) that says, "I don't even like you right now!" After a season of prayer, that same child may get up and cross the room to give you a hug and say, "I'm sorry I gave you a hard time earlier." That's when you realize that God's ways really are perfect, and all the effort we put into this process called homeschooling is more than worth it!

A LIFE WORTH FIGHTING FOR

At Wisdom's Gate, our family and staff gathers before the Lord for two hours each morning for a time of prayer and to "officially" start our work day by taking the time to unite our hearts and draw closer to our

God and to each other. It's a rare morning that we are not interrupted by something or someone! The enemy of our souls has been effectively using that old "divide and conquer" tactic for years and, near as I can tell, he's still up to his old tricks—and he doesn't have any plans to give it up in the near future, either! If you make a commitment to pray together as a family every day I can guarantee you—that old snake is going to come after you. If he can get you all going every which way and headed in different directions throughout the rest of your day, it weakens the fabric of your family as a whole, and it weakens the potential of each one individually.

No matter how "spiritual" the activity sounds, or how "important" it seems for you to attend, I learned a long time ago that a call on the phone is not necessarily a call from God. Now granted, sometimes there will be an immediate "knowing" in your heart, but you *still* respectfully submit it to the Father and say, "Should I go here or there and do this?" Just as you don't want your children marching up to you and announcing, "I'm going over to So-and-sos. I'll be back when I get around to it," neither is that how we should approach our God with opportunities that arise. We should humbly submit all these things to Him and trust His leading in all matters (Proverbs 3:5-6).

HOME SWEET HOMESCHOOL

Too many folks have yet to learn that running all over creation trying to get a blessing (or to *be* a blessing) is just not conducive to the establishment of a simple, Godly home-life and will considerably weaken (rather than strengthen) your effectiveness in raising Godly offspring.

Frankly, some folks approach homeschooling like life is just one big field trip! You ask your friend, "So, what are you studying right about now?" "Well, yesterday we were down the road and learned how they make antibacterial soap, and today we're headed up the road to watch the neighbor harvest corn and can tomatoes and, hopefully, we can get finished up early because tonight is the church volleyball game and tomorrow we'll be spending the day over yonder to see how they make candles..." In between the inevitable (and devastating) storms that come crashing in on them as a result of this misguided, whirlwind approach, before you know it, they're off to see the Wizard again! Then, they wonder why their children have ADHD, and their teenagers are freaking out, and things are not turning out as they had hoped! The truth of the matter is, they're not HOMEschooling!

If you are looking for a pattern by which to weigh the decision to participate in some activity, you've got to examine the fruit of it. When someone invites me to some gathering or activity, I immediately consider and observe the spiritual state of their young people. I'm looking for the fruit. Are they walking closer with the Lord and being drawn closer together as a family as a result of this activity? If it hasn't born Godly fruit in their lives so far—I'm certainly not going to lay my children on that altar! They'll be home safe with me that night. We might not do anything as wild and wonderful as what the world might be offering us, but my children will be in a good place. This incessant hyperactivity and constant running—every night you've got this meeting and that get-together, or there's somewhere that somebody in the family just *has* to be—is utterly undermining the peace and serenity that God intended for us as homeschoolers.

THE TYRANNY OF THE SCHEDULE

Another common mistake that leads to an overloaded schedule, and can result in burnout, is rushing to "cover the material" at the expense of understanding, or of being able to use the time for more profitable pursuits. "No, son, we've got to get through this. I don't care if you don't understand it. This scope and sequence chart says this is the day and now is the time so just get with the program!"

I know people that are just incorrigibly locked in to that spiffy daily planner (that they paid a pretty penny for). They are literally doing everything "by the book." Even if the child is actually getting interested in the lesson, "Boy, this is really fascinating how these math concepts fit together!" (Your child probably just said that this week, didn't he?) once the 45-minute time slot for that subject is over, all of a sudden these dutifully organized parents are saying, "Time's up! Let's just put that book away. It's time for us to move on to our phonics lesson." (I can hear someone laughing but, I've actually known people who homeschool that way!) I would strongly discourage that approach. Curriculum planners are wonderful tools as long as *you* use *them*—and not the other way around! (Besides, nothing grieves a child more than to find out he studied the wrong lesson and accidentally learned something he didn't have to!)

Learn to manage and incorporate your educational materials gracefully and responsibly. The "schedule" absolutely must never take the place of God in your life. If, at any point, that homeschool plan book becomes the supreme guiding force in your life then, by all means, put it in its place—and I do mean the trash can! Turn your heart to God and say, "What is it that *You* want me to teach these children today? What is it that they need most at this point in their lives?"

As Christians, we are to be led by the Spirit to follow the example of the Lord. Homeschooling is God's plan. It is not a tack-on to someone else's educational objective, or just an alternative approach to any number of educational options—*homeschooling is God's ultimate and best plan!* It was His original intention. Since He is the author of this plan, it makes perfect sense that you should allow Him to exercise absolute LORDship over your homeschool. I can't emphasize this enough. Allow nothing—or no one—to usurp His authority over your homeschool. Don't just give lip service and say, "Yeah, Jesus is Lord." Make absolutely certain that HE TRULY IS LORD! If you will be faithful in this one area, you are going to see changes for the good that you never would have imagined!

THE FREEDOM OF FLEXIBILITY

A flexible and realistic schedule is an absolute must for practical and effective homeschooling. Set a schedule that works for every member of your family.

Flexibility and moderation are effective tools that will help you avoid, at all costs, dead ritual and lifeless routine such as falling into the dreary pattern of learning "by the clock." (Do you know what I'm talking about? Pledge allegiance to the flag at 9am sharp. Math from 9:05-10:00, Science from 10:00-11:00, etc.) Instead, employ the Biblical model of teaching "as you walk by the way" and addressing important issues *as teachable situations arise* which means that, if Grandpa is demonstrating to your child how a root cellar is constructed, or Grandma is in the middle of explaining how folks back in her day kept their food cold all year round, trust me on this—strict adherence to the scope and sequence of your fancy (and probably very expensive) curriculum can take a back burner.

NO FEAR!

Fear of the unknown can be a trap for many homeschoolers. Most of us grew up in the government schools. It's what we know and became comfortable with. However, constructive change can bring new life to the old, dead bones of *modus operandi* and release us from the incapacitating paralysis of fear.

Let me give you an example…

We were renting a house one time and the furnace died and the landlord could not afford to fix the furnace so we were just kind of in a pickle. We tried to make the best of it, but we woke up one morning and discovered that the fish had frozen to death in the bowl. That's how cold it was in that house! (While we're on the subject, I'll tell you something else just to spare you a little lesson that I had to learn the hard way. In your sincere efforts to spare you children the trauma of such situations, don't try hiding the evidence by taking those fish to the neighbors and flushing those frozen fish down the toilet because they don't sink—they float!

You're going to have to scoop them right back out of there so, take my advice—don't even think about it!) Anyway, when I announced to the children, "We can't stay here anymore. It's too cold and we are going to have to move," they cried! "No, no! We'll just drink lots of hot water! We'll wear our snowsuits! No! Pleeease, Mom!" Can you believe it? They actually wanted to stay! It was unbearably cold in that place but it's what they knew. They had all their secret hiding places mapped out and their own turf established and they did not want to move—even if they were going to be the next victim to be found stiff in the morning!! (Thankfully, they submitted and we did move!)

Here's my point: for them, at the time, it was familiar and they were determined to cling tightly to it—*even if it was unrealistic, uncomfortable and not conducive to life itself.* We see the same ridiculous ruts in the road that some folks try to take in raising and homeschooling their children.

Fortunately, if you're walking with the Lord, He won't leave you in the desert wandering around in circles—He's got a Promised Land He's wanting to take us to and it's going to be good. No, we don't know the way, but He certainly does and that's why we follow Him. His stride is easily matched and His pace is comfortable and His course will always lead us in the right direction.

After years of scheduling overload, I have doggedly decided that *His* planner is the only one I will ever use.

What About Socialization?

It never fails. Sometimes it's while I'm trying to write a check at the head of a long checkout line, or while enjoying a picnic or family outing. It almost always happens when one of us appears as a guest on a radio call-in or TV talk show, or speak at a Wisdom's Gate Seminar or homeschooling convention. Whether in casual conversation or out of the blue upon learning that we homeschool, without fail, someone will inevitably ask the question, "But, what about socialization?"

The thing that never ceases to amaze me is that this question often follows an unsolicited compliment expressing the inquirer's favorable impressions of how nice, orderly, well-behaved, -mannered, -adapted, and sweet natured, etc. my children (or other homeschooled children with whom they are acquainted) are! So, what are these people so worried about?

In fact, these same "concerned" individuals are usually the ones who just spent the better part of an hour ragging on the social ills in the world today—and now they are wondering how your children are ever going to learn to be like the rest of the vile and ornery people they've just been complaining about?!

I'll admit there are definitely social skills to be learned down at the government schools that my children did not learn at home—such as how to sit on a hard chair for six hours without moving or talking, and raising their hands every time they have to go to the bathroom. But, frankly, most of the social "skills" I've seen exhibited by the average child who has been "socialized" by the government's institutional method are not exactly the meritorious traits in which I would prefer my child to be proficient.

SOCIALIZATION DEFINED

My dictionary provides a clue as to the real agenda behind the government school's compulsory attendance requirements with the following definition of "socialization": 1. To place under government or group ownership or control. 2. To make fit for companionship with others; make sociable. 3. To convert or adapt to the needs of society. 4. To take part in social activities.

Read it again. The point is, in our society, it is commonly accepted (though never formally announced) that our "OK" status is not official until it is judged and pronounced so by our peers. However, with an ever-changing standard whimsically dictating what is "cool," the attainment of general group acceptance presents a wearying task. Thus, peer-dependency is a root cause of burnout at any age level.

"Let us fix our eyes on Jesus, the author and perfecter of our faith Who, for the joy set before Him endured the cross, scorning its shame ... Consider Him Who endured such opposition from sinful men, so that you will not grow weary and lose heart" (Hebrews 12:2-3).

Peer pressure is not something we automatically outgrow. Regardless of age, we all feel pressure at one time or another to fit in, measure up, go with the flow or, somehow, qualify for acceptance. While peer *pressure* is normal and common to all, peer *dependency* is not. Likely, our motivation for wanting to somewhat "blend in" so as to avoid public scrutiny or potential conflict is rooted in fear. Remember, as we have seen, if not recognized and rejected, rampant fear can actually bring about the very thing that we fear the most!

"The fear of man bringeth a snare: but whoso putteth his trust in the LORD shall be safe" (Proverbs 29:25).

"I sought the LORD, and He heard me, and delivered me from all my fears. They looked unto Him, and were lightened: and their faces were not ashamed" (Psalms 34:4,5).

As homeschooling parents we have absolutely no Biblical admonition to "socialize" our children. However, *as mature Christians*, we are called to be salt and light to this world. Homeschooling is the process by which we prepare our children to fulfill that purpose. The erroneous notion that we should send our impressionable Christian children into those pagan dens of iniquity commonly known as "public schools" so that they can be "salt and light" makes about as much sense as dropping them off down at the local neighborhood gay bar so that they can be a witness for Jesus—and learn tolerance to boot!

As Christians, our goal should never be to "fit in" or blend together with a Godless society but, rather, to stand out and be separate. While many of us have come to understand that friendship with the world hinders our walk with our God (James 4:4), too many have merely shifted their eyes from left (the world) to right (fellow believers) rather than fixing their focus upward (Hebrews 11:2).

"Fear the LORD your God, serve Him only and take your oaths in His Name. Do not follow other gods, the gods of the peoples around you; for the LORD your God, Who is among you, is a jealous God and His anger will burn against you" (Deuteronomy 6:13-15).

Parental peer-dependency is simply the effective result of our own carnal nature exerting its deadening influence to keep us from growing in grace to reach our full potential and freedom in Christ. Yet, the uncontested Lordship of Christ requires our complete dependence on, and utter sufficiency in, Him alone.

So, do we just "hole up," bolt the door, reject fellowship and forsake evangelism? NO! We must seek wholeheartedly to know and desire Him, His will, and His way. Then, we must reach out in love toward others to encourage, equip and challenge them to focus on the same worthy goal.

LIKEMINDEDNESS

Rather than striving to measure up to the *status quo*, His Word must be our only standard. Then, when we come together in His will, we can compare notes and share proven methods and truths so that we all succeed in pleasing and serving Him.

The incessant quest for "like-minded" fellowship among Christian homeschoolers has brought grief and disillusionment to many a Godly family. If you search long and hard enough, you may succeed in finding a group of believers who look like you, dress like you, think like you, believe like you, and even, simply accept and *like* you—does that sound like heaven on earth?

Well, in the real world, circumstances and people change. Hopefully, we're all continually growing up and moving forward in Him. Yet, in reality, not everyone grows at the same pace. If "like-mindedness" is what brought us together, what is it that will keep us together when we find that we disagree on some issue?

Even more problematic—and far more insidious in its nature—is the fact that many of these groups of "like-minded" folks have based at least some of what they believe and practice on their preferences and traditions, and not necessarily on the Word of our God. Even if you are confident in your ability to stand up to the pressure, what about your children who have bonded emotionally and built strong relationships with other young people in the group which has become an intricate and intimately intertwined social circle? We've seen many families torn apart in such situations and devastated beyond remedy.

The only "like-mindedness" that should ever be pursued or can ever be embraced is when each one of us is unequivocally committed to lay down our own thoughts and agendas, and seek to fully possess *the mind of God* on every matter. That is the *Biblical* form of like-mindedness that our God can bless!

So, what will it be—"socialization" or Biblical relationships of blessing and encouragement?

"But, if serving the LORD seems undesirable to you, then choose for yourselves this day whom you will serve, whether the gods your forefathers served beyond the River, or the gods of the Amorites, in whose land you are living. But as for me and my household, we will serve the LORD" (Joshua 24:15).

PERILOUS TIMES

Have you ever been fooled by someone's slick propaganda? Have you ever thought that you were doing the right thing—only to have it blow up in your face? Have you ever thought that you knew someone—only to discover that he or she wasn't what you believed him or her to be? Have you ever thought that you could trust someone—and found out the hard way that the person was not worthy of your trust?

"And Jesus answering them began to say, Take heed lest any man deceive you" (Mark 13:5).

In this information age of "Storm Tracker" radar, and computerized satellite information systems, we humans may be tempted to believe that we have become like gods. Yet, some find themselves "in the dark" when it comes to discerning spiritual matters—many can't seem to see what is right in front of their eyes!

"O ye hypocrites, ye can discern the face of the sky; but can ye not discern the signs of the times" (Matt. 16:3)?

But, the times, they are, indeed, "a-changin'"! Things that were once unthinkable have now become the norm. Things once unspeakable have now become the regular fare of the daily news. Folks once would have scoffed at the idea of having to keep the doors and windows locked, and thought nothing of doing business on a handshake.

Now it is commonplace to have elaborate security alarm systems for our homes and vehicles, and lawyers on retainers. Some, who have "had enough" of the chaos of this age, are heading for the hills—and others are packing to follow!

How can we, as Christians, live in and reach out to this sick world, yet, maintain a safe and peaceful environment for our families? Is it possible to live purposefully and effectively for the Kingdom, or is life just a mere game of chance recklessly played against gambler's odds?

WISE AS SERPENTS

Though we, as Christian homeschooling families, may seek to walk humbly and live simply as separated from this world in which we dwell, that in no way implies that we may be simple-*minded*.

"The law of the LORD is perfect, converting the soul: the testimony of the LORD is sure, making wise the simple" (Psalm 19:7). *"The entrance of Thy words giveth light; it giveth understanding unto the simple"* (Psalm 119:130).

We're talking here about a life infused with a hearty dose of common sense, bolstered by Holy Spirit-inspired wisdom, and walked out according to Biblical principles—all of which translate into Godly actions and attitudes. A life lived in this manner leaves very little room for the enemy of our souls to enter in and have his way by bringing trouble, confusion and destruction into our lives. To merely shrug our shoulders and shuffle along aimlessly, denying the dangers and shunning responsibility for watchfulness will surely bring us to judgment.

"A prudent man foreseeth the evil, and hideth himself: but the simple pass on, and are punished" (Proverbs 22:3).

We must diligently endeavor to know and understand our God and to recognize the vast chasm between the holy and the profane. Rather than gobbling up the devil's lies and pigging out on the world's junk food, we ought to be feeding our minds on Biblical truth and feasting on the promises of our God.

"Strong meat belongeth to them that are of full age, even those who, by reason of use, have their senses exercised to discern both good and evil" (Hebrews 5:14).

The Holy Spirit is able and willing to enlighten us beyond our human capacity to know and understand all things, yet we must open our hearts to receive and embrace that holy insight which He longs to impart. If we are to truly walk according to His Will, and in His Way, we must strive to overcome our tendencies to live and act in a manner that "seems right" according to our faulty human logic.

"Trust in the LORD with all thine heart; and lean not unto thine own understanding. In all thy ways acknowledge Him, and He shall direct thy paths" (Proverbs 3:5,6).

Only God knows the future. Because the days are evil, we must do our utmost to exercise discernment in every situation. Unfortunately, the reality is, there *are* unscrupulous people in this world who are "out to get you!" That doesn't mean we should weird out like some folks who have crossed the line over into paranoia and tend to see disaster lurking behind every bush! Cynicism and skepticism are not virtues.

"Unto the pure all things are pure: but unto them that are defiled and unbelieving is nothing pure; but even their mind and conscience is defiled" (Titus 1:15).

Likewise, naiveté and gullibility are, also, not virtuous traits.

"Behold, I send you forth as sheep in the midst of wolves: be ye therefore wise as serpents, and harmless as doves" (Matthew 10:16).

We must walk carefully with our eyes wide open to see as far down the path as our human vision will allow—confident that, whatever lies beyond that point, our Heavenly Father sees and is able to handle. To give in to fear is to surely bring about our own undoing.

"The fear of man bringeth a snare: but whoso putteth his trust in the LORD shall be safe" (Proverbs 29:25).

While it is prudent to store up for the winter and to plan for the future, our confidence cannot rest in the works of our own hands, or the fruit of our labors. Our God, alone, is our Source and our Sustenance. He, alone, is our Shield and our Defense. He, alone, is our Rock and our Salvation. When it comes to socialization, *He* is the One that our children need to spend time with and get to know. The heart of the matter is simply this: where do we place our trust?

"Some trust in chariots, and some in horses: but we will remember the name of the LORD our God" (Psalm 20:7).

Whether by cloud in the day, fire in the night or bright star in the eastern sky—or, it may be through the power of His Word or through the *rhema* Word spoken by a friend—our God will speak to His people in order to lead, guide and direct them. If we will only just humble ourselves, soften our hard hearts, and listen, we will be spared much trouble and will be blessed beyond belief!

Homeschooling in the Light

Let's consider a few practical steps toward bringing Christian homeschoolers out of the closet and into the light while maintaining a solid focus and positive direction.

What do you think of when I say, "Ministry Outreach" or "Salt and Light"? Do you think of street preaching? Knocking on doors and handing out tracts? Dishing up donated gruel for the starving residents in the hot desert of a foreign land? Dropping Scripture balloons from an airplane? (Isn't that called "littering" in this country? Well, maybe it's different if you do it in the Name of the Lord...)

Ministry means a lot of different things to a lot of different folks. How can we best reach our world for Christ? How can homeschooling be incorporated into an effective ministry outreach? Maybe an even better question to start with would be ... what keeps people from reaching out to others with the substance of their lives?

FEAR OF REJECTION

Fear of rejection is a common factor—it is just in our nature to want to be accepted. Another reason folks don't like to talk to others about their relationship with Jesus Christ is because they don't have much of it to talk about. Fact is, some families are just barely able to "keep up appearances" and do not want to risk exposure of the fact that they really do not have it all together.

Perhaps, the most common reason is just selfishness and a lack of love for their fellow man. Servanthood is Christian love in work clothes. The Bible says, *"Greater love hath no man than this, that a man lay down his life for his friends"* (John 15:13).

Jesus is our supreme example when it comes to walking through life with that kind of love. He spent most of His life preparing to fulfill His purpose here on earth. His years in public ministry were few in comparison but, although many years have passed since He walked this earth, people are still talking about Him! The reality of His determination to do everything according to God's Will continues to impact people to this very day.

Even as we go about our day-to-day routine, anytime your family appears in public, you are making an impact on others—one way or another, for good or for bad. People are watching and noticing even the smallest things. Just the way your children carry themselves and interact with one another can have a great impact on people. The world is watching! The Bible makes reference to the fact that, whether on a church level or a family level, the world will be profoundly impacted by our loving example—they're going to exclaim, "See how they love one another!" You'll notice that it didn't tell us that they would be drawn to the *Lord* just because they may say, "See that great church building they're putting up down the road," or "What a great Christmas program those folks put on down there at that church."

The thing that will *really* impact people is *genuine, sacrificial, undying love.* That is what the world is hungry for. It's longing for it, it's looking for it, it's searching desperately for it. That part of the world that is truly seeking for something real won't run away from genuine Christianity—sane people don't run away from love.

Folks often approach us when we are out and about. They feel something in their heart that draws them. They don't react with revulsion, "Oh, no! Run away! Here come those people!" Instead, they'll come right up to us and somewhat shyly try to start a conversation. Sometimes, they will comment about our modest dress, but just as often they will speak of having noticed the love or joy reflected on the girls' faces or they'll remark about the obvious unity of our family or say something like, "I couldn't help but notice—your girls are just so sweet to each other." (Now, you need to understand, I'm bragging on the Lord here. We take no credit for anything good anyone sees in us. In His mercy, He has done so much for our family. That's how I know He can do the same for yours!) In reality, the girls do love each other and it shows. It's God's love that opens the door of opportunity for ministry to folks who have yet to truly meet and know our God.

FEAR OF CONTAMINATION

The fear of man will cause us to withdraw from healthy interaction and compassionate involvement in the lives of others who need to hear the gospel of Jesus Christ. Our lives will be punctuated by negative "what ifs" ("What if their children corrupt ours?" "What if our children are exposed to a lifestyle that differs from ours?" "What if we encounter a lion in the street?" Proverbs 22:13) rather than "why nots."

The fear of the Lord, however, will cause us to exercise appropriate caution with regards to our children while fearlessly reaching out to others in the Name of Jesus. It will move us to consider the needs of others over our own. It will propel us to action when our neighbor is in need. It will teach us to selflessly serve and not to pass unrighteous judgment on others.

Rooted in this problem of fear is a lack of confidence in our God to continue and preserve the work He has begun in us and in our children.

"Being confident of this very thing, that He which hath begun a good work in you will perform it until the day of Jesus Christ" (Philippians 1:6).

This lack of confidence in our God stems from unbelief. We simply do not believe in His promise to safeguard that which He has given to us for our good and His glory.

"For the which cause I also suffer these things: nevertheless I am not ashamed: for I know Whom I have believed, and am persuaded that He is able to keep that which I have committed unto Him against that day" (2 Timothy 1:12).

In the matter of academics, fear will cause us to censure our children's education rather than to guide and nurture it. Obviously, not all knowledge is expedient or profitable and I am not suggesting that you carelessly throw open the doors of your child's mind to all manner of evil exposure.

However, wisdom would indicate that a genuine and unshakeable Biblical worldview is gained by recognizing, understanding, and rejecting the vain philosophies and pursuits of this world in light of God's Word. If the foundation upon which we are building is truly one of conviction (rather than preference) we will not fear the fickle winds of opinions and false belief that blow about this world in which we live. We will have wisely prepared our children to boldly confront such nonsense when it presents itself once they are fully mature.

Now, you will notice that I said, *when* it presents itself, and not *if!*

In order to train up a child who can stand firmly in the presence of evil or temptation, you must adequately prepare them for anything that they may encounter along the road of life. Someday, your children will be out on their own and having to walk out those things which they have been taught under your watch. As much as possible, wouldn't you rather be there to instruct and support them the first time they are faced with an issue? If so, you had better be covering all the bases now, as you walk by the way, rather than hoping they'll be okay once they are grown and out from under your care.

Proverbs 22:6 will be successfully accomplished by balanced instruction and by practical example. As your children observe your own bold, mercy-filled ministry to those around you, regardless of the situation, they will learn how to walk in love and holiness among the peoples of this world without becoming soiled by such contact, or succumbing to the seductive temptations of a Godless environment.

APATHY

Perhaps, the most common reason for the lack of evangelistic outreach is merely selfishness and a lack of love for their fellow man. "As long as my family and I are getting by, those people can just fend for themselves!" If we had the love of God in our hearts, it would compel us to want to reach out to people. We wouldn't be sitting around fretting and *biting* our nails; we'd be out there *breaking* them in hard labor for the sake of a brother or sister that was in need. Remember, servanthood is Christian love in work clothes.

"Greater love hath no man than this, that a man lay down his life for his friends" (John 15:13).

Having considered a few of the hindrances to loving and effective outreach, we must stop and consider the most forgotten step in effective evangelism...

UPREACH BEFORE OUTREACH

The servant of the Lord must be willing to put in that time on his knees in prayer and intercession before the Lord, drawing from His well, before rivers of living water can flow out of him. Whatever is inside of us is going to come out—if it is good, and it's of God, it will prove to be a blessing to others. However, if you've still got a lot of worldly thinking and carnal, unregenerated flesh in there, folks are going to look at that and say, "No, thanks. I recognize that stuff. We've got plenty of that at home!"

Before we can impact the world we must intercede for those in need. When God opens your eyes to the needs of those around you, it's not because He needs you to open your *mouth* to the *ears* of others and blab everything you know about everybody. He is initiating dialogue between you and Him alone. He's saying, "Look at this! Look at these people. See the mistakes they are making and how they are suffering. Let's talk about this." He wants to open up to us His heart and His mind on the matter. Until you have the mind and heart of the Lord about a matter, you've no business jumping in with your physical presence or your advice. We have to remember that the battle is not being fought here on the planet. The battle is the Lord's and *He is always victorious.*

One of the main lessons homeschooling families need to learn is that…

IF YOU'RE WANTING TO REACH THE WORLD FOR CHRIST—STAY HOME!

Consider the example of our Lord once again. Jesus went about minding His own business (which meant doing whatever the Heavenly Father told Him to do—He had no agenda apart from that) and folks came to Him as He walked by the way, as He sat down, as He rose up. That is how He taught and won them. The people literally flocked to Him! In fact, at least one time, the press of the people was so great, He had to climb into a boat and shove out from shore just to get a little breathing space.

That is a far cry from what we see today! Look at the difference in the contemporary scene.

Today, in order to attract folks to their "activities," churches have gone to incredible extremes. Some are hiring professional marketing personnel to draw up advertisements that portray the church as being (and this is a quote) "non-condemning and user-friendly." This "come as you are, stay as you are" approach offers no real hope to the desperate and hurting. One church even used money out of their tithes and offerings to bring in the circus! Another sent out a flyer announcing their upcoming "Bible" school (though, I must confess, I have yet to find the following scenario in the Bible) that advised parents to have their children wear old clothes to church (here comes another quote) "where there will be face painting by the clowns at the church." (Look, folks, don't get mad at me. I'm not name-calling—that's their wording!) Think about that for a moment though—that is exactly what the world calls us; why would we want to give them ammo? The advertisement goes on…

"Meanwhile, the teens are all invited to participate in the paint balloon fight that will take place out on the church lawn." (I'll bet that really blessed the folks driving by!) The ad didn't say what the adults would be doing and I just shudder to think of the type of nonsense they are probably involved in!

To what are we attracting people with this kind of a process? How does any of this speak to a lost and dying world about Jesus? In what way are people being drawn to our God, or lifted out of their suffering, or called to forsake their sins and change their wicked ways?

The world is not impressed by these types of shenanigans. The bottom line is, *what has God called you to do?* If the Lord has called you to serve Him as a homeschooling Mom or Dad, why are you out running around doing all this other stuff? Charter Schools are not HOMEschools. Daily co-op classes and support group activities are not HOMEschooling. Has God really told you to be doing that stuff, or are you like Cain, just trying to come up with some alternative offering, "LORD, I know You said to do it this other way but, here, God, check this out. This is really cool and everyone is doing it and I just thought it would be so much more fun to serve You in this way."

You need to be standing consistently in your place fulfilling your calling to the best of your ability. In order to effectively disciple your children for the glory of the Lord, (which, if you have children, is *exactly* what He has called you to do) you need to be positioned steadfastly in your place wholeheartedly serving the Lord and your family. In order to train children at home, it's necessary for both the children and the parents to spend the majority of their time there—or at least, *together*. You can't train up and disciple children who are floating around the neighborhood, or running up and down the road, or hanging out down at the mall, or killing time over at a neighbor's house playing video games. If you find yourself wishing your family was closer, maybe you need to *be* closer, practically speaking.

Now, I'm not suggesting that you should never leave your house. There's a season and time for everything, but consider this: God desires for us to be like a city on a hill. A city doesn't run all over creation—it stays put in a specific spot. Everybody knows where it is and how to find it. It is certainly not hidden. Its light can be seen for miles. It is reachable (not out there in the ozones) and approachable (not a fortress designed to keep out fellow pilgrims).

Cities become known for certain characteristics. Philadelphia was called "the city of brotherly love." Chicago is known as "the windy city" (and, if you've ever been there, you know they got that one right). The Old Testament refers to places that were known as "Cities of Refuge." Think about it—what kind of city would your family be known as?

For you to be out trying to convince other folks of something that you have not yet personally experienced and incorporated into your daily life is like trying to be a door-to-door perfume salesman with nothing to show but a catalog! For a Christian to be effective, you've got to have the real thing and be ready and willing to show it!

Head knowledge alone is generally ineffective in bringing about deep and lasting change in the heart and life. So, as individuals and as homeschooling families, the majority of our time and energy needs to be applied to "walking the talk" so to speak. There's no better witness for our Lord than that!

"Let your light so shine before men, that they may see your good works, and glorify your Father which is in Heaven" (Matthew 5:16).

Separation from the World

"Be ye not unequally yoked together with unbelievers: for what fellowship hath righteousness with unrighteousness? and what communion hath light with darkness? And what concord hath Christ with Belial? or what part hath he that believeth with an infidel? And what agreement hath the temple of God with idols? for ye are the temple of the living God; as God hath said, I will dwell in them, and walk in them; and I will be their God, and they shall be my people. Wherefore come out from among them, and be ye separate, saith the Lord, and touch not the unclean thing; and I will receive you, and will be a Father unto you, and ye shall be my sons and daughters, saith the Lord Almighty" (2 Corinthians 6:14-18).

If you are serious about winning the world for Jesus, obedience to this command is absolutely imperative. Separation from the world is not an option—it is mandatory for everyone who names the Name of the Lord.

No matter how much of a facade you put up in front of people, sooner or later the real substance of your lives will show through. You simply cannot give away what you do not possess.

You hear a lot these days about Separation of Church and State. It seems that the mentality is that you can live peacefully with both as long as you keep them separate. The fancy term for that (in case you want to know) is *categorical departmentalization*. Personally, I just call it hogwash.

Folks, we're not talking about just keeping your blue jeans and your best white shirts separated into two wash loads—and then turning around and deciding it will be just fine to throw them all together in the rinse. If you set up a Godless government alongside a Holy

Church, there will always be a conflict—despite the fact that the two are totally separate. The truth of the matter is, the two are completely incompatible, and peaceful co-existence is utterly impossible!

For Christians, the call is not to "keep things separate" (like keeping your mud boots from getting thrown on top of your Sunday-go-to-meeting shoes—and then keeping those separate from your garden shoes, and your jogging shoes, and your golf shoes, and your bedroom slippers, etc.). No!

The only option we've ever been given is to *"come out from among them and **be** ye separate"* (2 Corinthians 6:17)! That is what it means to be HOLY. It means "set apart for a special purpose." You don't throw your good china in the cupboard along with the frying pans and paper plates. If you've got an heirloom silver pitcher you don't toss it out in the sandbox for the children to use to make mud pies or do science projects. That's because that pitcher is special. It has great value. Our lives have enormous value. We were bought with an incredible price.

Part of the problem is that, while there are countless millions who have never heard the Truth, here in America, we've heard it so much that we just take it for granted. Our hearts aren't filled to the brim with appreciation and our eyes don't overflow with tears at the thought that Jesus willingly gave His very life for us. We've heard it so much that, for far too many, it hardly means a thing—and I think that's why it doesn't mean anything to folks in the world, either.

Let me tell you once again—and don't just brush me off thinking, "Yeah, yeah. I know all of that." *Listen.* Think about this. Each one of us has been bought with the highest price that could ever be paid. Our life is not our own. The deal is, if you keep your life you lose it. If you lose it for His sake, it's yours forever. That's the offer (Matthew 16:25).

We need to reject this world's chintzy charm, turn away from its seductive enticements, and walk through each day set apart for His use. You can no longer just get up every morning and say, "Well, let's see ... today, I think I'll do this, and then I think I'll do that." No! You must get up each day and report for duty. You turn your heart to the Father and say, "Where do You want me to go today? What do You want me to do? Do You want to just stay here and fellowship together for a while? Yes, we can do that. I was fixing to start the breakfast dishes but yes, Lord, we can do that—we can stay here and talk for a while."

You must learn to walk every step of every day in close fellowship with your God. Remind yourself each day as you take up your cross (Matthew 16:24) that our Lord paid dearly for us to be His very own.

We belong to Him and, therefore, are under obligation to obey Him when He says, "Come out! Don't love the stuff of earth. Let go of the world and everything in it." Frankly, if you're not willing to do that—then you're just not worthy of Him.

There are plenty of religious-sounding, church-going homeschoolers who are headed into an eternity without Him. I know—because I was one of them! God knows full well that they spent their lives here on this earth doing what *they* wanted to do no matter how much they plead with Him in the end, "Lord, Lord, didn't we homeschool in Your Name?" He knows that they were only name-dropping His Holy Name like rock-star groupies who attempt to work their way into the "in" crowd by pretending to know a famous person they saw in concert once or twice.

Having His Word prominently displayed in your house means nothing if you don't have it planted deep in your heart and mind. His instructions must serve as the unshakable foundation upon which you build the spiritual house in which you live. His absolute Lordship and unrivaled dominion must encompass every area of your life. If He is not Lord of all, then He is not Lord at all!

Making the decision to come out of the world's educational system and accept your responsibility before God to train and educate your children at home was a good step. Homeschooling is a step in the right direction, but, it is only a step—and, one small step doesn't get you very far down the road.

He has a bigger picture. He died so that He might live (through us) so that the world through Him (by His atonement and, in a practical sense, as He reaches out to them through us) might be saved. If it's still *you* living this life, rather than Christ living in and through you, be honest—*you* are still on the throne of your life. YOU are the true lord of your life.

It's time for some of you to get off the fence and on to the straight and narrow path that leads to life. You're trying to live with one foot in the world and the other in the Kingdom of God, but the call of our Lord, as spoken by Joshua of old, is clear— *"Choose you this day who you will serve"* (Joshua 24:15a). I'm telling you here and now that I'm with Joshua— *"As for me and my house, we'll serve the LORD"* (Joshua 24:15b)!

If you start feeling overwhelmed and feel like you're drowning in the homeschooling sea, that's a real good sign that you just haven't climbed all the way into His boat. When Jesus is Lord of your homeschool you will find that His yoke is easy, and His burden is light.

If you really want to impact this world for Christ, I challenge you to leave it behind and *move*—move into the Kingdom. Have you ever had to move from one address to another? Did you send your friends and relatives a change of address card? Well, when you made the decision to leave this world and its lifestyles behind and move into the Kingdom, did you let all your friends and family know that you were going to be living forever as a stranger and pilgrim in a foreign land?

Let me ask you another question. Did you ever move into a new house and find that not everything you stuffed into that moving van and hauled along with you fit in your new home or lifestyle? If you've not done so in a while, I urge you to take a serious inventory of your life. In this day and age when *image* is considered everything, it may be difficult for some folks to comprehend the concept that we are not to have *any image but His*.

We need to dump anything and everything that does not reflect His image. Just get rid of it. Change your citizenship and let everybody know it. Burn your return passport. Put everyone on notice that you've accepted a higher full-time job offer that requires your permanent relocation. Don't make a way for yourself to pass back over that bridge—board it up! Claim the keys to a whole new way life, and settle fully and forever into the Kingdom of God!

If you are serious about reaching this world for Christ you must understand something—you can't reach *out* to something that you are still *in*! Some folks think you've got to hang out with the world and sample their goodies so that you can "relate"—or so that they can relate to you—but friends, that is a myth. If you're drowning in the middle of the same ocean as your neighbor, you won't be much help to him. You'll both sink.

Allow me to clarify something here. In speaking of our Lord's command regarding separation from this world, I'm not talking about some misguided, separatist, militia mentality that suggests we all should just head for the hills and hole up in the woods with our freeze-dried foods and ammunition. Separation from the world does not mean hiding out in the boonies where you don't have to see, or deal with, anybody (although we all have days where we would gladly settle for that interpretation)!

Separation unto the Lord is not a retreat—it is a forward momentum into the true light of day! Just as a young man will leave his parents and cleave unto his wife. Just as a wife moves from where she used to live, and places herself under her husband's authority. The two become separated unto each other, but they don't quit talking to, or caring about, folks in the world. We are separated unto the Lord in much the same way.

Have you ever been around newlyweds? They are in love and they don't care who knows it! It doesn't matter where you run into them—at church, at the market or the gas station—they just have that "glow." They're just kind of oblivious and detached from the world around them. Their wholehearted commitment to each other is obvious to everyone—and, that's just how it should be with every Christian who truly loves the Lord.

Since separation from the world is not optional for the true follower of the Lord Jesus Christ, what does it mean to be separated from the world? It means you don't feed your mind on the world's junk-food quality entertainment. You don't wear their uniforms or desire their bounty. You don't worship their idols or trust in their gods. You don't sacrifice your children on their educational altars.

By the grace of God, you will be able to walk in holiness through this life and keep yourself unspotted from the world. Don't worry about the risk of becoming so Heavenly minded that you're no earthly good. You are in far greater danger of being so contaminated and weakened by the things of this world that you're of absolutely no use to the eternal purposes of a Holy God.

Meanwhile, for those who want to argue that God only looks on the heart and doesn't care about externals, in one sense it's true—holiness is definitely a matter of the heart. True holiness is most truly reflected in the actions of a heart that has turned itself totally and completely toward serving a *holy* God.

If you're willing to lay down your life, and your personal preferences, and say, "Not *my* will but Thine be done" as He did, I promise you that, by the grace of God, you will be able to walk through this life in holiness and keep yourself unspotted from the world.

Holiness is not popular in our day but you must come to understand this truth beyond a shadow of a doubt—holiness is not optional; the Bible says, without it, *no man will see God* (Hebrews 12:14).

That's a heavy price to pay for a cheap, fleeting dance in the arms of the world.

Servanthood: Being Salt and Light

With our lives in order and our homes firmly established in place as a solid base of operation, we can then begin to look about us and watch for opportunities to reach out in the Name of the Lord to a needy world.

Christianity has been studied and practiced for ages but, unfortunately, it has been studied more than practiced. You may have heard me say it before: from what I've observed, it's not always a matter that the majority of folks in this day and age are merely rejecting our God. Often, they're rejecting hypocrisy. They're rejecting a powerless form of Christianity. They're rejecting people who say one thing and do another. They're rejecting a type of Christianity that talks in King James vernacular but lives like the devil. I am convinced that most folks who remain outside the Christian camp are simply saying NO to the mock version of Christianity that shamelessly parades itself through the streets, businesses, schools, homes and churches of our day. I believe that many in this world are simply choosing, instead, to hold out for the real thing!

The truth of the matter is, the world is literally *dying* to meet our God. They're tired of seeing so-called Christians who go to church on Sunday and pray to, and sing songs about, "Our Father" and then run around acting like orphans the rest of the week. They're longing to experience the love of a family and the security of home.

As Christian homeschooling families, that is something that we can show them. The Godly fruit born out of a Biblical approach to homeschooling will be manna to those who are still wandering without hope in the wilderness.

A close-knit, loving family can have a powerful impact on the world. The world needs to see that toddlers can sit still and behave themselves for periods of time when necessary. The world needs to see that children can get along and love one another. The world needs to see young people who respect and obey their parents. It needs to see young ladies that aren't boy crazy and young men who still have honorable intentions. It needs to see that the teenage years do not have to be traumatic, and that growing pains are something that teenagers experience—not something they are!

Never are these traits more beautifully displayed than when the family is shod with the shoes of servanthood. We should always be on the lookout for practical ways to reach out as families and share the fruit of our lives with others. The possibilities for outreach are endless and the fruit yielded for the effort is so rewarding.

Nursing homes are excellent outreach opportunities for families to minister together. Both the residents and the workers will be touched by your unified outpouring of love to the elderly, many of whom have been abandoned by their own families.

Hand-made crafts such as homemade soaps, bread or cookies (hardly anyone bakes cookies anymore!), are great homeschool projects and make excellent gifts for any occasion—or no occasion at all.

Housecleaning for the elderly or sick is a practical and appreciated labor of love in which even young children can participate.

Hospitality is commanded in Scripture and is a wonderful way to touch hearts as you open your own hearts and home to those the Lord brings your way.

Besides being a blessing to those you serve, these opportunities for service will have a powerful impact on your children as well. Any opportunity to serve others helps to bring children outside of themselves and nurtures a servant's heart.

There was a time when a man's success was measured by how many servants he had, but in the Kingdom of God, true success is measured by the number of folks a man serves. Most any businessman can tell you that it is faithful, excellent service that brings success.

Some folks struggle with the concept of servanthood—especially those who have embraced the modern day, play-baby mindset. ("Those children shouldn't have to work like that!") Entertainment, vacation, and retirement are the buzzwords of our day. If the concept of servanthood is new to your family you may even meet with some resistance from one or more of your own children.

SERVANTHOOD: BEING SALT AND LIGHT

We can certainly understand their struggle. All around us, athletes, actors, singers, and even politicians—many of whom do not even acknowledge the existence of our God—are being presented with monetary awards and glittering trophies, and showered with praise and honored with applause while the cameras roll and the world looks on approvingly.

Meanwhile, there are no lights and cameras, no news reporters on hand, and no one calling you up to sing your praises as you arrive home exhausted after spending the day wading in cold sewage sludge up to your ankles, with your throats burning for lack of fresh air, while trying to salvage the moldy contents in the basement apartment of a crippled and elderly widow whose home has been flooded by a malfunction of the city sewer. (By the way, this woman was a long-time member of a large church and yet, by her own admission, "could not think of anyone else to call who would be willing to come and help except for that homeschooling family that everyone knows has helped folks out when they were in need." What a blessed testimony!)

Servanthood is not a glamorous calling, but let's face it—it's better to be the tail on a live dog than the head on a dead one. Amen?

A WORD OF CAUTION

We've all met parents who think their children are so "bright" that you almost feel you ought to wear sunglasses when you are around them. While our God told us to *"Let your light so shine before men"* (Matthew 5:16a), don't blind folks to the blessings of homeschooling by constantly bragging on your children. If you will simply allow the light of the Lord to shine through you, He has promised that folks will, indeed, *"see your good works and glorify your Father in Heaven"* (Matthew 5:16b).

Let me just mention something here. Don't feel that you always have to be shining the light on the shortcomings of others by continually ragging on the government schools, or comparing your children to their classroom-educated counterparts. I would heartily agree that the government schools are riddled with problems. No matter how many ways they try to package it (Remember Goals 2000? The School to Work Program? No Child Left Behind?) government schools are just the mouse race that prepares young folks for the rat race.

If folks aren't coming hungry and asking honest questions, there's just no sense trying to force-feed them the answers. Better to just keep on stirring your own pot and when that sweet-smelling aroma that emanates from your humble home reaches them, they'll take a candid look at their spiritually emaciated offspring and find the courage to come knocking on your door. When that happens, you'll be ready to reach out and receive them in the Name of the Lord because you've been faithful to quietly *do* all that He has commanded, and not merely talk about it.

BEING SALT AND LIGHT

If you, as a family, are walking with God, hearing His voice as He promised we would, doing His Will as He asked, you won't have to go out and evangelize by knocking on doors, and handing out tracts. Folks will come to you! In fact, more than likely, you'll be having to worry about things like how you're going to get in and out of the market and back home in time to fix dinner without somebody stopping you to ask questions. While many will be content to just stop you as you go by, some folks are so hungry that they'll go to great lengths to seek you out—even showing up on your doorstep. Of course, you'll be there in your place, stoking the home fires so that when the road-weary, worldly travelers are finally ready to come in out of the cold, they'll be drawn by the beacon of light that shines from your heart's window. They'll come to you and say, "I'm sorry to be so bold but, I've heard about you and I just had to know more. What makes your life so different from the rest?" Then, you can just invite the person in to be warmed by the fires of His love as you sit down with your family at your own table to break the Bread and not only *"pass* the salt," but *be* the salt of the earth, as well!

Again, we are called not just to witness, but to *be* a witness—that's 24/7 whether we ever open our mouth or not. When folks can recognize Him living in and through us, we will be His unspoken message to the world. Rather than being put off by us, folks will be drawn to us as weary, storm-tossed sailors who desperately search for the welcome security and peaceful stability of the old landmark lighthouse standing faithfully along the shore. It is in this way that we will truly and effectively fulfill His command to be "salt and light" to a world that flounders aimlessly in utter darkness. He truly is a faithful God and a rewarder of those who diligently seek Him (Hebrews 11:6).

BEFORE LONG OTHERS WILL SEE THE LIGHT!

We talked earlier about the fact that God desires for us to be like a city on a hill. This is Lifestyle Evangelism magnified and multiplied—

I'm talking about a city with some real candle power—a city centered in the Kingdom of God, which our Lord explained to us is not of this world.

This type of witness becomes a reality when one person hears God's call and says to himself, "I believe that there is a promised land." Then, turning to his brother, he says, "I believe that, together, we can make it to that good land." Before long, others catch their excitement and begin to pack up their bags and still others start moving a little closer so their lives can be touched by what God is doing and, ultimately, the substance of *their* lives will have a positive impact on the Kingdom, too.

Folks often refer to the Christian homeschool movement as "the homeschooling community." We're not talking about a hippie commune or a kibbutz, but Biblical Christian community. That city on a hill that is made up of individual families who share a common goal. That's what *we* mean when we talk about community: "Common Unity"—sharing things we hold in common in the Lord as we follow His leading in our lives; not only taking personal responsibility for our own individual lives, but caring about the lives of others as well—this is Kingdom living at its finest!

It's time some of you wake up and realize that you're still living in Egypt—and God is calling for an Exodus! We absolutely must shake ourselves free and reject everything that this world has to offer. We must find or create a nurturing habitat—an alternative and truly Christian culture where each member of our family can be rooted to bloom and grow and bear fruit that will outlast this sin-riddled world. We're talking here about the true church—and I don't mean The First Church of Saint So-and-So down on Such-and-Such Avenue. This is the genuine and living church—sanctified and set apart for the Master's sake.

Let me remind you, I did not come to know God until I was in my mid-30s and had absolutely reached the end of my rope. Up until that time, although we were church-going folks, doing the whole religious routine (Sunday morning and evening service, Sunday School, Bible School, Youth Group, etc.), we were as lost as lost can be. Our family was a wreck and life was an endless nightmare from which we hoped we would someday wake up, and yet feared that we never would. I simply cannot fully describe for you how my children suffered in their early life. There was *absolutely no hope*. No joy. In fact, our life was so bleak that, even at five years old, one of my little ones had never once laughed. Never laughed! Can you imagine? The first time she laughed out loud, we all broke down and bawled!

Considering the fact that, when I first met the Lord, about 17 years ago, I had six children (from babies to teenagers) to raise as a single mom, we've basically all kind of grown up in the Lord together. As the fruit of our life in the Lord began to ripen, we began to reap a harvest that was beyond our wildest dreams. I saw the fruit of God's mercy in the lives of all my children. I saw genuine joy on their faces for the first time in my life! It just made me weep! I never could have believed that I would ever, *ever* have lived to see the day when God would do for me what He did for us in setting us free from the effects of sin—and in showing me His plan for raising my children by simply bringing them up in the nurture and admonition of the Lord as we walked by the way, and sat at His feet, in the context of homeschooling. True to His Word and by His mercy, He has restored those years that the locust had eaten (Joel 2:25). We have tasted and seen that the Lord is, indeed, very, very good (Psalm 34:8).

So, please don't think, as we share our testimony throughout this book or at our seminars and tell what God has done for us, that we think we are too cool, or better than anybody else. Our purpose in sharing our testimony of God's grace toward us is not to try to get you to be like us—it is to encourage you to be like HIM! It is only when folks recognize Him living in and through us that we will be effective for the Kingdom as emissaries of His unspoken message to the world.

I hope that you are using the time spent with this book to quiet your heart before the living God. Do some honest soul-searching and ask yourself if you have a firm hold and a solid grasp on everything that you are longing for, and needing to receive, from the Lord.

In fact, why not just take a few minutes to close your eyes and forget about everyone else for a moment (assuming the children are safe and under control!) and just stand spiritually open and attentive before the Lord for just a moment as you ask yourself these questions...

Would your family be known as a City of Light? Are your relationships at home in order? Are you dwelling together in peace and unity? Can you rejoice knowing that all the children God has placed in your household are walking in truth? What (or whose) image would people say you project? Is Christ living in and through you each and every day, or are you still in the driver's seat?

Hear my cry, O God; have mercy on me and grant the desires of my heart to raise children who will bring glory to Your Name. Amen.

Teaching The Truth

"Then said Jesus to those Jews which believed on Him, 'If ye continue in My Word, then are ye My disciples indeed; and ye shall know the truth, and the truth shall make you free'" (John 8:31-32).

Just yesterday I was asked again a question which has been put to me many times, "How do you do it? How can you manage to hold on to faith against all odds? How can you maintain such a steadfast hope in the midst of such adversity?"

Truth be known, humanly speaking, when it comes to trouble, I am a basic coward. My tendency is to want to run headlong for the hills whenever trouble strikes. I hate conflict and can't stand fighting and haven't the stomach for strife. Were I merely left to live according to my own human tendencies, I would be the worldwide, undisputed, Queen of the Wimps!

But, even greater than my dread and abhorrence of conflict is my deep love of the truth. You see, it was the TRUTH that ultimately set me free from a relentlessly miserable life of sin. It was the TRUTH that brought light to my darkness and showed me the path of righteousness that is leading me surely and safely to my eternal Home.

THE TERRIBLE BONDAGE OF STRONG DELUSIONS

This world has been duped by the slick representatives of the enemy of our souls. Many, even in the churches, have been deceived into believing that the Word of our God can be twisted around to mean anything at all—or merely ignored altogether!

Our God warns us that we will live to see the day when some who believe themselves to be good people will actually succumb to the sinister trap of strong delusions and be given over to believe a lie (2 Thessalonians 2:8-12). The reason this happens is because they "love not the truth" that could save them from such an awful predicament.

Once this delusion has taken hold, the person is a captive who is no longer free to think rightly and see clearly. If you have ever encountered this situation in a friend, loved one or acquaintance, you know that it is almost impossible for anyone to help such a person. The frightening thing is, once this happens, the only thing that can save that person is the very thing which they have foolheartedly abandoned and willfully continue to reject—TRUTH!

"And ye have not His Word abiding in you: for Whom He hath sent, Him ye believe not. Search the Scriptures; for in them ye think ye have eternal life: and they are they which testify of Me. And ye will not come to Me, that ye might have life" (John 5:38-40).

As in Jesus' day, modern-day Pharisees are especially vulnerable to this spiritual malady. These are those that have a form of Godliness—they may look, dress, and even sound spiritual—but they deny the power of God that is able to overcome their spiritual pride and self-righteousness, and deliver them from their imagined, exalted state. We're talking about church folks now, mind you!

"This know also, that in the last days perilous times shall come. For men shall be lovers of their own selves, covetous, boasters, proud, blasphemers, disobedient to parents, unthankful, unholy, without natural affection, trucebreakers, false accusers, incontinent, fierce, despisers of those that are good, traitors, heady, highminded, lovers of pleasures more than lovers of God; having a form of Godliness, but denying the power thereof: from such turn away. For of this sort are they which creep into houses, and lead captive silly women laden with sins, led away with divers lusts, ever learning, and never able to come to the knowledge of the truth" (2 Timothy 3:1-7).

A BIBLICAL STANDARD OF TRUTH

Many times over the years certain well-meaning individuals have come along and suggested numerous ways that we could adapt our approach to become more "mainstream" and make our ministry less "emotionally threatening" and more "user friendly."

No one, they say, wants to hear about "outmoded concepts" such as obedience to God's Word, respect for parents, love of siblings, simple and sacrificial living, walking by faith, responsibility and accountability, humility and mutual submission. Terms like modesty, purity, and chastity have become novelties in our day. Biblical standards, Godliness and holiness are archaic notions to our modern culture, we've been told.

As a result, obviously, books such as this one and magazines such as *Home School Digest* and *An Encouraging Word* will never be popular among the masses because Jesus is not popular, and the Scriptures that point the way to Him are even less popular. No one wants to *"deny himself, and take up his cross daily, and follow"* (Luke 9:23) any agenda but his own.

It has become increasingly obvious (in this age of "tolerance" and "no absolutes") that our Holy God and His Word of truth are two sure things that *absolutely* will not be *tolerated!* So we are not taken by surprise when we find ourselves faced with opposition and taking the heat for our politically-incorrect message and stance on the controversial issues of our day.

The reason we are able to persevere without compromise in the midst of adversity is because there is nothing we've ever faced in this life that our God did not warn us about in advance and promise to see us through—and nothing of which Jesus is not aware or has not, Himself, experienced *and overcome.*

Because I have found Him to be totally trustworthy and His Word to be *totally true*, there is nothing that I can ever encounter here in this life that will be able to shake my faith in Him or cause me to doubt His goodness or deny His powerful truths.

There is no other path that I would ever be willing to walk—no matter how lush and promising it looked—if I could not see Him leading directly in front of me every step of the way.

I agree wholeheartedly with our Brother Wayne Watson when he says,

> "I'd rather walk in the dark with Jesus
> than to walk in the light on my own.
> I'd rather go through the valley of the shadow with Him
> than to dance on the mountain alone.
> I'd rather follow wherever He leads me,
> than to go where none before me have gone.
> I'd rather walk in the dark with Jesus
> than to walk in the light on my own."*

(**Walk In The Dark*, lyrics by Wayne Watson. © 1993 Word Music (ASCAP). All rights reserved.)

HOW TO TEACH THE TRUTH

As homeschooling parents, our goal is not to produce politically-correct citizens but, rather, to train up our children for the glory of God and for fruitful service in His Kingdom. The wisdom of this world will never accomplish this task, but by God's grace and our faithful, Godly example, we will succeed in our mission by adherence to His Holy standards.

We have little ones in our care who will be following after us even as we follow after Jesus. As we seek to be faithful in training our children in Godly character let us be diligent to instill in them a love of the truth as is taught in the Scriptures which will enable them to truly have the mind of Christ and His Spirit of humility.

"Let nothing be done through strife or vainglory; but in lowliness of mind let each esteem other better than themselves. Look not every man on his own things, but every man also on the things of others. Let this mind be in you, which was also in Christ Jesus: Who, being in the form of God, thought it not robbery to be equal with God: But made Himself of no reputation, and took upon Him the form of a servant, and was made in the likeness of men: And being found in fashion as a man, He humbled Himself, and became obedient unto death, even the death of the cross" (Philippians 2:3-8).

Let's be careful to apply this mindset to our homeschooling so that we are not turning out little Pharisees who think they have the truth and are, therefore, somehow superior to others when, in reality, they are guilty sinners who were born needing to be saved by God's grace just like the rest of us.

We can learn much from the examples of others along the way.

"Now all these things happened unto them for ensamples: and they are written for our admonition, upon whom the ends of the world are come. Wherefore let him that thinketh he standeth take heed lest he fall" (1 Corinthians 10:11-12).

However, once you think you know it all you are no longer open to the truth because you think you have arrived and are in possession of all the knowledge that you need—a dangerous position, indeed!

THE FREEDOM AND WISDOM OF HUMILITY

Humility engenders a life-enhancing teachableness that will serve us well throughout our course here on this earth and will protect us from the pitfalls of pride and the mire of selfishness from which there is little hope of escape aside from genuine repentance according to His mercy.

Only the truly free can walk through this life with courage and boldness and yet, recognizing the limitations of their humanity, readily and sincerely speak the words, "I could be wrong," "I welcome your input," "I'm open to correction," or, "I've made a mistake. Please forgive me."

Hard hearts and hard heads seem to often reside within the same bodies. The surest protection against being carried away and enslaved by the merciless bondage of deception—including *self*-deception—is to maintain a humble and contrite spirit whereby the Holy Spirit is able to deliver you from the isolating chains that are formed by the deceitfulness of satan's lies, and from the cold, dark prison of false belief and wrong assumptions.

Despite what any and all other homeschool families are doing, if you desire above all else to succeed in raising your children according to God's standards, you must establish a holy habitation where His unflinching, unwavering, absolute truth will reign in your home. When His thoughts have become your thoughts, and His words have become your words, when your steps fall directly into His footprints along life's road, when the only voice you will ever heed is His and His alone, you will be set free—no longer a slave to fear—to face life's trials and to live each day in joyful victory, come what may. Now, that's the truth!

Hands-On Homeschooling

A Godly approach to homeschooling takes into consideration each child's abilities, learning styles, interests and talents. So what did everyday homeschooling look like at our house?

We are often asked to define our educational philosophy or describe our approach to homeschooling. When *TIME* magazine interviewed us a few years ago, they chose to categorize our family as "THE UNSCHOOLERS." (That bold label appeared in their article on homeschooling under a halfway decent picture of us taken in our 4000+ book library—I guess maybe they thought we were using all those books to provide extra insulation and soundproofing throughout the house.) Well, at least it gave our friends a good laugh to think of us as "unschoolers." Anyone who spent even one day around here definitely would not call our homeschooling style "relaxed"! While we are certainly not "traditional" in our approach to education, I guess I would define our educational approach as "natural" or "real-life" education that is very focused and purpose-driven while remaining flexible and not unduly structured.

Trying to determine a practical direction for each one of my children has been challenging because every one of them is so multi-directional in their talents, abilities, interests and areas of expertise. Out of all six of my children, no two are alike. They all have different strong points—and weak points. Each has a different learning style-auditory, visual, kinesthetic, hands-on, etc., or (with most of them) a combination of two or more styles, so I have sought to establish opportunities for learning that enhance the natural abilities of each child yet serve to correct their inherent negative traits or tendencies.

For example, Israel, my son, a hands-on, auditory learner, who overcame dyslexia and hyperactive ADD, has always been involved in some kind of media whether print or broadcast. He talked incessantly at the age of two so it seemed quite natural that, as a 15-year-old, he developed and hosted his own radio talk show "Teen-to-Teen" which he successfully pitched and marketed for broadcast on several stations. Israel does most of our radio interviews and provides soundbites for national news stories. He has developed his own recording studio where he produces professional quality CDs, audio books, and inspirational messages. Israel is often featured as a keynote speaker at homeschool conventions and teams up with me at Wisdom's Gate Seminars. Now a published author in his own right, he has written the popular book *Homeschooling From A Biblical Worldview* and is a regular contributor to our publication *Home School Digest*. Currently, in his spare time, he serves as the Marketing and Media Director at Wisdom's Gate. All of this has given him experience in management, media relations, marketing/advertising, manufacturing, publicity, print publications, creative writing, public speaking, and so much more. He and his sweet wife Brook (who was completely homeschooled as well) have several precious children and an active home life, as well.

However, Israel is not the only one of my children who has prospered through the approach to homeschooling we have practiced and shared with you in this book.

Several years ago, under the direction of an experienced builder who willingly serves in a variety of needed ways at Wisdom's Gate, my girls built a beautiful 20- X 40-foot addition to our place [algebra/mathematical calculations, carpentry, teamwork, FAITH!] partly to house the quality resource library we've been developing (in our spare time!!) which covers history, gardening, biographies, cooking, and how-to books on just about every subject [library science].

I've heard my mom say many times (quoting her grand-mother in reference to progress), "Sometimes, it has to get worse before it can get better!" Still, I was more than slightly intimidated by the thought of digging the Michigan version of the Grand Canyon in my front yard and ripping a gaping hole in the side of my house—all in the name of progress, of course—so that the girls could get a little hands-on learning experience. Yet, as a parent I learned a long time ago that, in order for them to really learn, there are times when you just have to get out of the way and give the younger generation a go at it. They worked hard at delivering quality craftsmanship and their loving servanthood is reflected in the finished product. It truly was a learning experience—for all of us!

Hopefully, our approach to homeschooling will not conjure the stereotypical tomboy image of girls who try to be like boys. My daughters are certainly "ribbons and lace" type of girls who are well-balanced and strong enough emotionally to jump in and work hard or get dirty or break a fingernail (without crying over it) whenever the need should arise. They are definitely strong (in body and in the Spirit), but they are not rough and hardened by any means!

Remember, from the time we enter this world we are continually learning. There is nothing that anyone is capable of doing that they did not learn to do somewhere along the way. Although we have applied ourselves strategically to formal/traditional forms of study (textbooks, tests, reports/essays), most of our education has come from a practical, hands-on, real-life context rather than from a textbook. High school graduation has never been held as the ultimate goal for these youngsters. We understand that to live is to learn. Learning is an inseparable part of our lifestyle.

The traditional testing/grading system can leave a child with a wrong impression of what learning is all about—as if memorization of rote facts or getting top grades is the ultimate goal. However, striving for academic excellence for the purpose of eventual, practical application toward effective service is a worthy objective that converts mere "head knowledge" into "wisdom"—and wisdom is something you just can't get out of a textbook. (As a business manager, I've encountered many a college graduate who came with papers in hand looking for a job yet lacked common sense for even the most basic applications.)

In our case, Wisdom's Gate Ministries has provided our family with the perfect balance between hands-on learning and practical application in the form of service. All of us have labored together to embrace the Lord's vision and fulfill His plans for the long-term focus and operation of Wisdom's Gate. Meanwhile, there are currently about a dozen phone lines to keep up with, endless company expenditures to co-ordinate, and the need to develop marketing and promotions strategies for our product line including our quarterly publications, *Home School Digest* and *An Encouraging Word*. This has provided first-hand learning opportunities in management, media relations, marketing/advertising, pre-press production of print projects including the layout and design of our publications, catalogs, advertising, promotional pieces, etc. Couple that with the website design and maintenance [artistry, graphic design, computer, photography] and you can see that there is plenty of opportunity to develop and employ creativity in the areas of graphic design and technical expertise.

The girls have all taken part in the everyday operations of the ministry which includes such varied positions as, managing our warehouse and shipping department [management, budgeting, organization] and processing phone and mail orders and thousands of E-mail each month [postal operations, public relations, purchasing], reading, writing, proofreading, transcription, database management and subscription fulfillment [typing, data entry, computer skills, clerical, public relations], coordinating travel arrangements and scheduling itineraries [publicity, public relations]—at times, it seems the list is endless!

Besides the home service opportunities and apprenticeship applications mentioned above, the girls have overseen our small farming operation over the years. Here they gained experience in landscaping and gardening—which, one year, included planting over 200 pine and maple trees, blueberry and strawberry plants plus, perennials, herbs, flowers, etc., installing a 16- X 20-foot goat barn and spacious run, and putting in 5,184 running foot of protective fencing for their free-range chicken operation [math, finances, farming, animal husbandry, veterinary skills, botany, science, carpentry]. All of the children are gifted musically and have often been invited to play and sing together for local events [music, performance, service].

Since the girls recognize the possibility of having their own homes and families someday, they presently apply themselves to every aspect of home management. We bake our own bread, and cook from scratch [food service, nutrition, budgeting]. (Each of them is experienced and fully capable of single-handedly planning, preparing and serving a formal breakfast, brunch or dinner for 30!) We've learned to make our own soap and taught ourselves the basics of embroidery and crochet [homemaking/domestic skills].

Spiritual counseling [discipleship] and hospitality [servanthood] to visitors from all over the world are a major part of the daily life at Wisdom's Gate. The character traits of self-discipline, personal responsibility, cooperation, faithfulness and more are developed in all of these endeavors.

I know many young people who are wondering what they are going to do with their life. Honestly, now that I think about it, I've never heard my children complain that they were bored! Once, one of my girls commented that she wonders how—even if she lives to be 100—there will ever be time to do all that she would like to learn to do! Even at my age, I can really echo those sentiments.

(For the record, lest it sounds like it's all work and no play around here, we all still managed to find time for playing on the trampoline, friendly competition in softball and volleyball, participating in music fellowships and activities with friends, sunset walks along the beaches of Lake Michigan, and holding marathon Scrabble matches!)

Despite the diverse interests of our educational direction, instilling strong moral character was always a primary goal of our educational focus. Even more important than "head knowledge" is "heart wisdom." Our God has warned us that knowledge alone will only tend to make a person prideful (1 Corinthians 8:1). Without moral character, all the "book-learning" in the world will not equip a person for true success. We've all known brilliant, gifted men and women who ended up losing everything, or even landing in prison, because they lacked moral integrity.

We are well aware that a child who has spent his youth centered in himself will not make a good servant in the Kingdom of our God. So, to us, education—regardless of its depth and scope—is incomplete unless a person has learned to do whatever it is they do with humility and integrity, and a spirit of cooperation in working together with others for a purpose outside of themselves.

Because we are very busy, as a defense against self-centeredness, we make an extra effort to make ourselves available to others when a genuine need arises—such as helping to pack and load a moving truck for a friend, or preparing meals and cleaning the home of someone who is sick or injured, lending a hand on a friend's building project, or helping to get the neighbor's crops in before the rains.

Jesus taught that those who want to be great should strive to be the servants of all. If the sum of our learning equals a better quality of life not only for ourselves but also for others, then we will be truly successful. If, in the process of all our learning, we master the ability to "love our neighbor as ourselves" we will have learned something of real value.

Definitely a "hands on" homeschool project.

A lesson in ingenuity... No ladder? No problem!

Guitar practice

Preparing Children to Serve as Unto the Lord

The training of our children must always be done with their future service to the Lord in mind. If we have been diligent to deliberately instill Godly character that manifests itself in every area of our child's life, upon reaching maturity he or she will be choice vessels ready for the Master's use in any context in which He may desire to place and use them in this life.

If a child has not mastered and manifested desirable character traits in his interaction on the home front, he will not possess or demonstrate such attributes in his adult life.

A child who has spent his youth centered in himself will not make a good husband or father or employee. A young man who has continually shown callous disregard and deliberate disrespect to his mother or sisters while growing up will not be entirely competent to cherish his wife or dwell with her in an understanding way (1 Peter 3:7).

A young woman who has never evidenced a lifestyle and heart-attitude of sacrificial servanthood will not be wholly prepared for the incessant demands inherent to the responsible management of a household.

Any child who has been even mildly successful in cleverly manipulating his parents and siblings in order to get his own way will, by brazenly hiding the truth, bullying or guilt-tripping, or in other cunning ways shirking responsibility, inevitably use those same tactics on his wife.

Children who have not learned to submit to one another in the fear of the Lord will find themselves unwilling and/or unable to defer to others and yield their will in selfless consideration of a spouse.

From their earliest years, a child must come to understand one foundational truth: "It is not about me—it is all about Him!"

TAKING INITIATIVE

A child who has been properly trained will be zealous to do anything that is necessary for the orderly operation of the home setting in which he is raised. His earnest aspiration should be to honor his parents and to bring glory to his God in whatever he does and says. He is sensitive to the needs of others and ever alert to opportunities to serve.

On the contrary, the one who constantly waits to be told what to do has not fully matured so as to be willing and capable of voluntary, responsible service. As a result, unless this character trait were to change, he would not be deemed a fitting tool in the Hand of the Lord.

It should be carefully noted that the taking of initiative does not constitute a running ahead without waiting on clear direction from God. Neither does it comprise a jumping in and doing that which seems right in the child's own eyes impervious to the need for wise counsel. Initiative is not to be confused with impulsive behavior. Prayerful initiative leaves no regrets.

"Trust in the LORD with all thine heart; and lean not unto thine own understanding. In all thy ways acknowledge Him, and He shall direct thy paths" (Proverbs 3:5,6).

Once a child has learned to come under authority, he should be expected to take conscientious initiative to begin to walk out that which he has been taught.

Godly initiative is characterized by the taking of appropriate action based on confident application of learned truths tempered by prudent understanding. It is equivalent to the difference between a son standing securely and functioning freely in his place, who learns to enthusiastically and meaningfully participate in the convention and order of his father's house, and a lazy, insensitive slave who hovers cringingly in the shadows on the outskirts of the social circle hoping he won't be summoned and called into service.

FULLY MATURE

While it is true that the fear of the Lord is the beginning of wisdom, it is only the beginning—a first step, if you will, toward a much greater fulfillment of His plan. If fear continues as the only motivation for our obedience to Him, then we have not reached the full stature of maturity that is characterized by perfect love (which casts out all fear). We do not truly know Him as our Father.

In the same manner, if the only thing you ever accomplish in raising your children is to instill enough fear in them to keep them from disobeying your direct instructions, you will have failed to fully accomplish your task. You have not truly succeeded in bringing them into the beautiful fullness of relationship that is distinguished by a loving eagerness to serve and to please you through a willing and enthusiastic submission to your expressed will ("Son, do not allow the dog to run loose after dark") and perceived aspirations. ("The weather forecast predicts that it will not rain all week and I know Dad would not want the newly sown grass to die in this heat wave so I must remember to turn on the sprinklers while he is away from home on business so as not to disappoint him.")

Those positive characteristics, when achieved, will carry beyond mere obedience to an enterprising effort to comprehend and perform that which would prove to be a blessing to others. Rather than cowering self-protectingly or being resentful of your authority, your child should come to wholeheartedly embrace all that you have sought to impart. Once this has become a reality, you will have established a life-long relationship in which you can expect to experience cherished, loving and joyous fellowship throughout your lifetime together.

A GENUINE WITNESS IN THE WORKPLACE

In order for you to fully equip your child for any area of service to which the Lord may call them, you need to give comprehensive consideration to possible future scenarios and weigh your child's potential performance in light of their present manner of conduct. Carefully examine the fruit of their lives as it is borne out in contemporary situations and applications.

For example, if your son has no aspirations toward becoming an entrepreneur then he will, most likely, be engaged in the employ of another to whom he will be held accountable. Furthermore, regardless of his vocation, he will also be held accountable by a Higher Authority to Whom he owes even greater service. Therefore, your satisfactory training of him would, of necessity, anticipate and include the following considerations (to examine just a few).

"Servants, obey in all things your masters according to the flesh; not

with eyeservice, as menpleasers; but in singleness of heart, fearing God: and whatsoever ye do, do it heartily, as to the Lord, and not unto men; knowing that of the Lord ye shall receive the reward of the inheritance: for ye serve the Lord Christ" (Colossians 3:22-24).

As a Christian servant, an employee must work just as hard when the boss is away as they would if he were standing there looking over his shoulder, and will encourage others who work around them to do the same.

Dawdling, laziness, carelessness, murmuring, gossiping about the boss or other employees, borrowing (or stealing) supplies provided for use on the job—all of these have no place in the life of a true Christian.

Promptness, attention to detail, paying heed to instructions—all these show proper respect for the authority of the employer and express, in a practical way, appreciation for the position which has been offered and accepted.

While the unbeliever may view his employment as "just a job" to be endured for eight hours a day, the Christian will offer his wholehearted participation throughout each and every business day and will work for his boss as diligently as he would work for himself or, more importantly, for the Lord Himself.

"Let nothing be done through strife or vainglory; but in lowliness of mind let each esteem other better than themselves" (Philippians 2:3).

The Christian will not be always looking for personal reward or advancement, but will seek to apply himself in such a way that the company or person he works for will gain a reputation for excellence regardless of whether or not he gets the credit.

"Likewise, ye younger, submit yourselves unto the elder. Yea, all of you be subject one to another, and be clothed with humility: for God resisteth the proud, and giveth grace to the humble. Humble yourselves therefore under the mighty hand of God, that He may exalt you in due time" (1 Peter 5:5-6).

Witnessing for the Lord should be done through the shining example of a life well-lived—especially when the employer's time clock is ticking away. Lunch hour and break times may provide opportunities for spoken witness and sharing of Biblical truths.

The Christian will demonstrate his integrity and trustworthiness by always giving his best to his employer so as to never cheat him in any way—particularly not in time, resources, honor, or money.

God will reward the employee who, in all these ways which we have mentioned, is faithful to serve his Master (by wholeheartedly serving his earthly master).

Obviously, this is by no means a comprehensive list of considerations, but you get the picture. This strategic and God-directed approach to training is easily applied to any number of life-situations for which your child may need to be prepared.

As you prayerfully seek the Lord with regards to the unique and eternal purpose of each of your children, our God will be faithful to lead you and guide you in the course you should take in order to properly prepare them for a life of fruitful service. With the right goals clearly established, you will have no trouble "hitting the mark" when the time comes to release your "arrows" in the direction the Lord would have them to go.

"Lo, children are an heritage of the LORD: and the fruit of the womb is His reward. As arrows are in the hand of a mighty man; so are children of the youth. Happy is the man that hath his quiver full of them: they shall not be ashamed, but they shall speak with the enemies in the gate" (Psalm 127:3-5).

WALKING BY FAITH

What are we teaching our children—by word and by example—about the Christian disciple's wholehearted servanthood in His Kingdom? Lasting change (transformed living) comes by the renewing of our minds (Romans 12:2—which is also part of the process that makes knowing and doing the will of the Lord possible). Remember that part of His ongoing work in us is to cause old things to pass away and all things to become new (2 Corinthians 5:17). Therefore, I challenge you to prayerfully consider the thoughts that I am sharing with you so as to broaden your understanding and deepen your commitment, and to abundantly equip you to train up your children as profitable servants in the Kingdom of our God.

How can we teach our children to learn to walk on their own by faith? The answer to that question is simple: we teach them by example—one step at a time! Here's how the faith walk has played out in our own lives...

By my mid-30s, I had spent my life on the typical American lifestyle of selfish and meaningless pursuits and had nothing to show for it in light of eternity. When I met the Lord Jesus, I gave my life completely over to Him at that time and purposed to hold nothing back for myself. From that day to this, His will and His Kingdom have been my reasons for everything I do.

Realizing that no one can serve two masters, and that this life passes very, very quickly, I separated myself from the world—as He requires of anyone who would truly be His disciple—and began the walk of faith with Him that has now become Wisdom's Gate Ministries.

All of us who serve the Lord full-time at Wisdom's Gate have left our nets (former worldly ambitions and employments) to follow His leading and to be ready tools in His hands to accomplish His will. One benefit of this is that it allows us to make disciples of our children even as we labor to disciple others—with our children working right alongside and seeing firsthand the goodness and faithfulness of our God.

As servants in the Lord's household we trust the Lord to meet our needs—which He has always been faithful to do. (If you have studied the life of George Mueller, you will be familiar with the realistic application of this Biblical concept.) We do not encumber ourselves with the world's system or ways any more than is absolutely necessary or required. (We use the things of earth but do not allow them to use us.)

Most of us have intentionally and carefully positioned ourselves so as to be able to serve the Lord full-time without having to concern ourselves with the pursuit of "gainful employment." In other words, our days are no longer consumed by "trying to make a living"—rather, our purpose has shifted from "getting" for ourselves to "giving" of ourselves. We freely go wherever He sends us and do whatever the Lord places on our list each day trusting Him to supply our legitimate needs as He has promised to do.

On a practical level, we are able to do this by living simply as servants in His Kingdom, and not as purposeless consumers in this world. We have worked hard to downscale the world's demands on our lives and to become debt-free so that our living expenses are very minimal. Our motivation in choosing this way of life, is that we have been able to avoid the dilemma of trying to serve two masters and, so, have complete liberty to be always immediately available and directly accountable to our Lord Who purchased us with His blood and to Whom we wholly belong.

I am often reminded of the words of the songwriter, "Oh, Jesus, Lord and Savior, I give myself to Thee, for Thou in Thine atonement, didst give Thyself for me. I own no other master, my heart shall be Thy throne, my life I give henceforth to live O Christ for Thee alone."

The work of the Lord that our God has called us to here is simply one of many opportunities in this world to cast down our nets, lay down our life, take up our cross and forsake all to follow and serve the Master. Only a remnant will ever truly obey His call to this level of self-sacrifice. Especially in this country, I know very few people who are able (or, more precisely, willing) to live this way, but for me, I truly know of no other way to live in Christ—and He has blessed our life in Him abundantly!

On a horizontal level, the work is ruthlessly demanding, dizzyingly relentless and, for the most part, a thankless enterprise. However, we do not labor for earthly praise or reward in this life knowing that our Lord is a just and fair Master, and everything done in His Name and for His sake will carry over from this life and be credited to our account in eternity where our imperishable treasure is being stored up for us daily. Thus, a life work that would be viewed as a worthless drudgery to some according to this world's standard of measure continues to be a source of unspeakable joy and blessed fulfillment to us.

For someone who is used to drawing a substantial paycheck and may be accustomed to, or dependent on, a high standard of living (monetarily) and the "security" of such perks as insurance, IRAs, paid vacations, etc., the reality of walking out life as we know it could be a bit of a shock!

If you have a desire to find a place within the context of full-time Christian service in which you and your family can serve Him, you stand facing similar choices as I faced seventeen years ago when, as a newly born-again single mother of six children (ages infant to teen), I cried out to the Lord regarding my deep desire to find a place within the context of Christian ministry in which the children and I could learn and grow to serve Him together.

For over fifteen years now, I've been teaching/discipling others toward knowing Jesus intimately and walking in obedience and close fellowship/communion with Him as His children/disciples and citizens of the Heavenly Kingdom (and, therefore, no longer of this world—John 17:16). Having made my choice long ago, and with the faith of those days now having turned to sight, I stand a good bit farther along on the pathway and, so, am able to out hold this lantern of faith to show you the way.

However, I would insert a word of caution here. It is important that any decision you make regarding what you will do with your life be based on your strongly-held conviction in response to His clear call on your life in that direction. You can't walk out anyone else's faith—you will only stand accountable for your own. So, the first step is to discern the Lord's call. The second step is to set about to know what we must do to accomplish His revealed will in and through us confident that, *"faithful is He Who calls you—and HE will do it"* (1 Thessalonians 5:24).

If you seek to walk in faith, money absolutely cannot be the draw with regards to—or the hindrance to a faithful response to—the clear call of God. Once our God has clearly revealed His will in a matter, we must move forward with confidence and resolve knowing that we serve the God Who is able to "make a way where there is no way"!

As I mentioned before, long ago, I answered a call to work for the Lord in His fields with no guaranteed income and to trust Him to provide for us because we have wholeheartedly and willingly laid down our lives to follow Him and give Him not only the first-fruits of our lives, but our all. From that perspective, all of us here have answered a missionary call to serve the Lord as disciples/followers/servants rather than merely viewing our position as "working for a ministry."

The Lord's provision may come from our primary place of service or it may come as gifts from other sources. Our purpose for being here is not to draw a paycheck although we may regularly receive a certain amount from the Lord through resources drawn from this ministry, or provided unexpectedly as gifts from other sources as a result of His faithfulness in supplying our needs according to His promises and as recompense for our service to (and faith in) Him.

In fact, most of us here believe in the rightness of what we are doing through this ministry to which we have been called to the point that, if need be, we would go out and get night jobs to pay the bills (and even to generate funds to cover the work of the ministry) so as to continue to work for the Lord just as we do now. The true test of whether or not you are serving the Lord or man (or yourself) is simply this: if you were not getting paid to do what you are doing, would you continue to do it only because it is what our God has called you to do?

Just as when I explain in our magazines that, "Wisdom's Gate is owned by the Lord Jesus Christ and operated under the guidance of the Holy Spirit" the concepts that I am laying out before you here are not merely a game of semantics. This perspective towards our labor is fundamental to our life in Him. By the same token, we recognize that *all* funds (not just a tithe) that come in to the ministry belong to the Lord and His work, rather than as belonging to ourselves. Therefore, we are extremely frugal in our lifestyle drawing only a minimal base amount as is necessary to cover our basic needs.

In this world, it's all about money—without question one of the premier gods of this world—but, in the Kingdom, it's all about our God. With every encumbrance of earth, we are decreasingly able to serve the Lord freely and effectively. Personally, I wouldn't trade the glorious freedom we have in Christ, as citizens of His Heavenly Kingdom, for ownership, possession, and control of all the stuff this world has to offer—and the bondage that comes along with it!

Our Lord was very specific regarding the things that would be the undoing of our faith—*"the cares of this world, the deceitfulness of riches, and the lusts of other things entering in, choke the Word and it becometh unfruitful"* (Mark 4:18-19). This is the essence of the battle between heart and mind, that affects each one of us. We have His Word imprinted on our minds and hidden in our hearts but everything we hear and see in this world out-shouts and seemingly outweighs His promises to us. In this manner, our profession of faith is tested and what we *really* believe becomes manifest.

Children will remember your manner of life as it was walked out based on your strongly-held convictions (or the lack of them) long after the daily course work of the finest curriculum has faded from memory.

May our God grant you the grace to lead your children—by word and by example—to walk through this life by faith in Him based on the promises of His Word.

Training Stewards for the Kingdom

How do our children perceive the love of God as it is communicated through our present stewardship of the Lord's resources?

With regards to the Lord's provision, if the life we live in this body is going to be pleasing to the Lord, we must learn to live lives of faith (Hebrews 11:6) as children in the Father's house. Your children probably do not know (or, at least, do not have to know) what your financial situation is, what your budget requirements are, etc.; as children, they are carefree—which is exactly how the Father wants *you* to be (Mark 4:18)! You can be responsible (spend wisely, live frugally) without being obsessed (approaching financial matters as if you are, or must be, the one in control) with finances.

Especially in America, where older folks can still remember what is known as The Great Depression, there is a strong emphasis on the need to save up our pennies for a rainy day. The concept of saving for the future makes sense—there's certainly nothing wrong with being prepared for emergencies. However, as stewards of the Lord's resources, is it really right for us to assume that everything that passes through our hands belongs to us? Isn't it likely that a portion of the supply that the Lord sends our way is meant to be passed along to bless others who are facing *immediate need* rather than hoarded against the *possibility* of a need that may arise somewhere down the road?

"Hereby perceive we the love of God, because He laid down His life for us: and we ought to lay down our lives for the brethren. But whoso hath this world's good, and seeth his brother have need, and shutteth up his bowels of compassion from him, how dwelleth the love of God in him? My little children, let us not love in word, neither in tongue; but in deed *and in truth"* (1 John 3:16-18).

One of the surest ways to guarantee you will never run short of supplies for the necessities of life is to refuse to hoard resources in the face of manifest need but, rather, to freely—and even sacrificially—share with others as the Holy Spirit leads you.

"Give, and it shall be given unto you; good measure, pressed down, and shaken together, and running over, shall men give into your bosom. For with the same measure that ye mete withal it shall be measured to you again" (Luke 6:38).

One thing to keep in mind when considering such matters as saving for the future is the commandment of our Lord in Matthew 6:19-21: *"Lay not up for yourselves treasures upon earth, where moth and rust doth corrupt, and where thieves break through and steal: But lay up for yourselves treasures in heaven, where neither moth nor rust doth corrupt, and where thieves do not break through nor steal: For where your treasure is, there will your heart be also."*

It is so easy to forget that the eternal God is our source—especially with regards to such matters as saving for our children's college education or future. If we are not careful, our children may grow up with a tendency to look to *us* as their supply. However, if we have truly done our job as parents/disciplers, by the time they are grown and are beginning to step out into lives of their own—whether it be missions, marriage or considering furthering their education through college—they will have established enough of a relationship with our God that they can go directly to Him for funding of any venture undertaken according to His will. Regardless of the direction He calls them, He will meet their need—and their *greatest need* at that point is to walk responsibly and intimately with Him through the process. If it is not His will for them to go to college, they would obviously be remiss to waste that portion of their lives in vain pursuit of that which does not please Him and from which He has withheld His blessing—possibly even in the form of financial support.

"Take therefore no thought for the morrow: for the morrow shall take thought for the things of itself. Sufficient unto the day is the evil thereof" (Matthew 6:34).

Our purpose, in the meantime, is to see to it that their relationship with Him is genuine and secure. What better preparation—for life and eternity—can we offer our children than to introduce them to the God of the Universe; the God Who created and owns every good and perfect thing in this world and Who is in control of all things? When your children come to know the Lord as *Father* through the relationship they observe between Him and their earthly father (and/or mother), when they have witnessed the Lord do the impossible in their lives, when they have cried out to God with their own voice and watched Him send so much food to your door that there is hardly room to store it all, or have seen Him heal the sick and raise the dead right before their very eyes, confidence in Him will come easy to them because He is no longer just someone they know *about*, He is Someone they personally *know*! Genuine relationship with our God is the ultimate inheritance that parents can leave for their children and their children's children. (Proverbs 13:22-25; Psalm 103:13-17) A man (or woman) cannot leave a greater legacy than this.

Deuteronomy 10 and 11 have much to say to parents about the Lord's requirements, provisions and promises and are excellent Scriptures to study deeply and prayerfully. In addition, our Lord's teachings in Matthew 6 are foundational for those who have come to fully comprehend the truth of the "missionary concept"—that we travel through this life here on this earth as strangers and pilgrims in a foreign land. *"For here have we no continuing city, but we seek one to come"* (Hebrews 13:14). Therefore, this world being no longer "our home," our status changes from "citizen" to "missionary." No matter where we find ourselves on the planet, we are only there as ambassadors on a mission to do the Lord's will and work.

"Therefore I say unto you, Take no thought for your life, what ye shall eat, or what ye shall drink; nor yet for your body, what ye shall put on. Is not the life more than meat, and the body than raiment? Behold the fowls of the air: for they sow not, neither do they reap, nor gather into barns; yet your heavenly Father feedeth them. Are ye not much better than they? Which of you by taking thought can add one cubit unto his stature? And why take ye thought for raiment? Consider the lilies of the field, how they grow; they toil not, neither do they spin: And yet I say unto you, That even Solomon in all his glory was not arrayed like one of these. Wherefore, if God so clothe the grass of the field, which to day is, and to morrow is cast into the oven, shall He not much more clothe you, O ye of little faith? Therefore take no thought, saying, 'What shall we eat?' Or, 'What shall we drink?' Or, 'Wherewithal shall we be clothed?' (For after all these things do the Gentiles seek:) for your Heavenly Father knoweth that ye have need of all these things. But seek ye first the Kingdom of God, and His righteousness; and all these things shall be added unto you" (Matt. 6:25-33).

Food and clothes are the easiest part of financial planning because our God has told us not even to write them into the list! He has specifically promised to cover those things and so we trust Him to do so and spend no mental energy ("take no thought") trying to figure out (as the gentiles do) how we are going to come up with those needed items. The Father knows that, as pilgrims and strangers living in a foreign land, we have need of all these things and has promised to take care of His household. We will not insult Him by lying awake worrying about how we are going to cover everything in case our Heavenly Father does not keep His Word!

So, in the truest sense, a budget is a record of what we are in the habit of spending, not an amount that we need to come up with to survive. Our primary focus is not to be on the acquisition of *things*, but on what we need to do to qualify for cashing in on those wonderful promises our God has made to us. The answer is found in Matthew 6:33: *"Seek ye first the Kingdom of God, and His righteousness; and ALL these things shall be added unto you!"*

I could look back over recent years and tell you how much our family has spent on food, clothes, etc., and about the genuine miracles He has performed in our behalf, but that would only tell you what our God has done for *us*. I can testify to the ways He has been leading us through the years and how He has directed our paths, but we don't have a system or formula for guaranteed financial success other than those Biblical truths and principles that I have touched on in this book. If you were to take our budget figures and try to arbitrarily duplicate our spending patterns in your own household without the clear leading and direction of the Holy Spirit, it would probably fail.

We have only one thing with which to be concerned—we must seek to please the Lord in all we do. *"O fear the LORD, ye His saints: for there is no want to them that fear Him"* (Psalm 34:9). Fear of anything but the Lord is not faith.

If all things are spelled out for us in advance to the minutest detail, it no longer is a walk of faith, is it? Faith in God will always be rewarded! God wants you to seek Him directly for even the minutest details of life so that He can be LORD of all that pertains to your life. I can only tell you what is possible for a people who, in faith according to His Word, are wholeheartedly serving the God of the impossible. It is your responsibility to turn to the Lord in these matters and say with the Apostle Paul, "Lord, what will You have me to do?"

In the early years, the Lord made it clear to me that I was not to continually watch the finances (even in checking the records to see how many magazine subscriptions we were up to). I was to leave that all with Him and just do what He showed me to do. If we need or want something, I ask the Lord and if He says I should buy it, I buy it. Many times, He has said WAIT and I have had the blessing of seeing Him bring it to me as a gift! The key is not to try to figure it all out for ourselves—we just need to turn to our God, acknowledge Him in all our ways (Proverbs 3:5-6), and trust that He will direct our paths.

As we daily deny ourselves, take up our cross and follow Him, we concern ourselves only with obedience to His will and that subject constitutes the majority of our petitions before Him. Financial issues, which at one time were so prevalent in our thoughts, often remain unspoken in prayer simply because there is no need to voice them (Matthew 6:7-8). The truth is, we hardly think about such things but, rather, keep our mind on higher things and find, whenever we pause to reflect or look back at the end of another busy year, that our God has always more than supplied our needs—exceedingly, abundantly, beyond what we could ask or think (Ephesians 3:14-21)!

If our supply dwindles, and our petitions are denied, our God, Who knows the heart of man so well, may simply be testing us (not so that He can *discover* what hides in our hearts, but so that He can expose our true motives as *we* are brought to face the deceitfulness that lies buried within each one of us). He knows whether we are really asking to be debt free so as to be totally free to serve Him or if we are asking so as to be able to consume it on our own lusts (James 4:2-3)—i.e., we want the security of "owning" and feeling like everything is under control (ours) or maybe we still have insatiable cravings for the stuff of earth and will turn around and accumulate more stuff and more debt. He knows that, in that case, in our hearts and minds, it's all about us and really not about Him at all! In such a case, it would not be in our best interests for Him to grant our requests and further feed the appetite of SELF that is reigning within us. The Father knows whether our requests will supply a genuine need or merely cater to our flesh and pamper a selfish want.

In a country overflowing with material blessings it can be difficult to maintain a proper perspective and balance between genuine needs and frivolous niceties or mere conveniences. If we are not careful, we may easily come to love God's gifts more than the Giver of the gifts.

"Give me neither poverty nor riches! Give me just enough to satisfy my needs. For if I grow rich, I may deny you and say, 'Who is the LORD?' And if I am too poor, I may steal [to steal is to speak with our actions that our God cannot be depended upon to keep His promises to supply our needs] *and thus insult God's Holy Name"* (Proverbs 30:8-9).

Consider our Lord's instructions through Paul in First Timothy

6:8-12: *"But, Godliness with contentment is great gain. For we brought nothing into this world, and it is certain we can carry nothing out. And having food and raiment let us be therewith content. But they that will be rich fall into temptation and a snare, and into many foolish and hurtful lusts, which drown men in destruction and perdition. For the love of money is the root of all evil: which while some coveted after, they have erred from the faith, and pierced themselves through with many sorrows. But THOU O man of God, flee these things; and follow after righteousness, Godliness, faith, love patience, meekness. Fight the good fight of faith, lay hold on eternal life, whereunto thou art also called, and hast professed a good profession before many witnesses."*

Hopefully, you're able to glimpse here a Kingdom-eye-view, if you will, of living peacefully and securely in God's economy. Should you decide to obey His call to wean yourself from dependency on the things of this world, when you are tested at some point down the road (as you surely will be!) if you have only arrived at your decision to walk by faith in every area of your life including the matter of finances merely because you have been convinced by facts and figures (things which can be shaken) that it is a smart thing to do, then you will be found among those things that can (and will) be shaken. (Hebrews 12:22-29) But if you have stepped out in obedience and solid faith to follow the leading of the Lord, when the test comes, you will not cave in to doubt, discouragement, or fear but will stand strong through the test and see the salvation of the Lord as He delights in showing Himself strong on behalf of those whose trust rests only in Him (2 Chronicles 16:7-9).

So, how is it with you, my friend? Is yours a walk of faith? If you were to lose your main source of income, would you panic or despair? In word and in deed, in what (and in whom) are you really teaching your children to put their trust?

I pray that our testimony will encourage you to walk confidently in Him knowing that He will not lead you where He cannot keep you. Lay your family, lifestyles and finances before the Lord and allow Him to help you to see your handling of His resources through His eyes based on His plans for you—and make any necessary adjustments accordingly. You will never regret having put your trust in Him!

"For the LORD God is a sun and shield: [He provides blessing and protection] *the LORD will give grace and glory: no good thing will He withhold from them that walk uprightly. O LORD of hosts, blessed is the man that trusteth in Thee"* (Psalm 84:11-12).

May our God have reason to bless you!

Learning to Let Go

In homeschooling circles, courtship and betrothal have become quite popular. More and more parents are taking their responsibility seriously by ordering tapes and reading books and articles on the subject.

Many are even taking time out to attend weekend seminars devoted to understanding the spiritual and practical dynamics of sexual and emotional purity, and exploring the ways and means of getting their offspring safely to the marriage altar.

A PROBLEM OF MAJOR PROPORTIONS

Despite this zeal for a better way to approach relationships, a problem of major proportions has arisen which is having disastrous effects on these otherwise well-meaning families.

While increasing numbers of young people are coming to the marriage altar with hearts and minds prepared to enter this new phase of life, too many parents are failing to prepare themselves for the day when their children will leave them to follow the Lord's leading and fulfill His purpose for their lives. To explain this situation in a nutshell: parents do not seem to know how to gracefully and graciously let go.

I've seen so much damage done to relationships between parents and their married children simply because the parents will not exercise the self-restraint to bring themselves to stand in a proper place where they can allow their children to obey the Biblical command to "leave and cleave."

HOW DO THINGS GET SO MESSED UP?

Parents who, themselves, may have been raised in less than ideal circumstances by parents of another era (who, although they may have meant well, were also not properly trained to do their job and, therefore, made more than their share of mistakes) might flounder about confused as to how to go about this ever-evolving task of parenting their children at every stage of life.

While our God has plenty to say about this matter of training and releasing children, parents who have not fully surrendered to God in other areas of their lives will not be able to surrender to His will, no matter how obviously revealed and confirmed, in the matter of their children, either.

GIVING IT OVER TO GOD

I know countless parents who rallied all their deductive reasoning skills and searched far and wide using an exhaustive, systematic grid to find "the right person" to meet all of their physical specifications, economic requirements, doctrinal criteria and character qualities—and they, and their child, have lived with regret ever since.

The difference, as I see it, is a matter of who is in control. When we allow God to choose our children's mates (rather than hyper-controlling the process in our limited knowledge and understanding) we will find that His ways really are perfect and His plans are so much better than anything we could ever conceive or implement.

From start to finish—from birth to marriage to the grave—whatever call God would place on the lives of their children, parents absolutely must come to the place where they are willing and ready to *let go and let God have His way*. The will of the Heavenly Father should always trump the will of an earthly parent (Acts 5:29). Whose children are they, anyway?

EMOTIONAL INCEST

One possible problem that may present itself is that the natural affections of the parents may be out of balance and inappropriately directed toward their children. If our love for God is not as it should be, our love for our children cannot be what it should be either (Deuteronomy 6:5).

Husbands and wives who have failed to properly develop and nurture their own relationship may have, unknowingly, begun to emotionally attach themselves to the children in an unhealthy way. The prospect of being left alone with a stranger in an empty nest once all the children have flown the coop may result in feelings of panic which cause the parent to react to a natural pattern and course of events (which God established and ordained since the beginning of time) in an unnatural and unGodly manner.

Single parents may also be vulnerable to these feelings of loss and need to guard their hearts to make certain that they know, beyond a shadow of a doubt, that Jesus really is all they need and to take steps to ensure that their lives really are centered in and around Him—not on their children.

AN ISSUE OF CONTROL

The issue of letting go is especially problematic in cases where the parenting style has been one of dominance (heavy-handed authority that is self-motivated and out of balance with Scripture) rather than a parenting style that was focused on equipping the young person to walk with increasing devotion and dependence upon their God.

A child raised in this environment may passively abide by the rules, but the child has never come to hold to the standards of the household out of personal conviction because he or she has never been allowed that choice.

This child has simply not been properly or Biblically trained up in the way he should go. He has merely been controlled by a power outside of himself (the parent), rather than from within as a result of a heart and mind that has been renewed through the counsel of the Scriptures and the power of the Holy Spirit through the nurturing of Biblically-based parenting.

Once the adult child is out from under the parents' authority, by reason of age, maturity, marriage or calling, he or she may begin to make choices that may displease or even shock the parents (Luke 2:42-50) who may, then, wrongly react to what they perceive as a sudden rejection of themselves or their values when, in reality, this may simply be the first opportunity the child has ever had to express his true feelings, views or beliefs and prove what is really in his heart.

SELF-DIRECTED PARENTING

Many parents have merely taken the bully's approach to parenting. Rather than taking the time to gently instruct and train the child—

line upon line, day after day, as they walked by the way—the parent has simply "laid down the rules" and then proceeded to "rule" with an iron hand. Self-directed parenting says, "I'm the boss around here. You'll do what I say because I said so!" rather than, "In this house, we do certain things because our God has instructed us to walk this way and we are all accountable to Him."

Parents who have raised children by this self-inflated parenting style will not have a healthy and prosperous relationship with a grown child who is no longer under their control and has begun to make a life separate and apart from their authority.

Regardless of the issues, parents who find themselves in a power-struggle with their married children need to examine their hearts and repent of anything that does not conform to the Word of God or yield itself to the control of the Holy Spirit.

THE TRANSFER OF AUTHORITY

While there is much that married children can glean and learn from their parents, had God intended an authoritative hierarchy, He would have specifically instructed children of all ages to obey their oldest living grandparents and to live under their roof so that they could maintain control, but this tribal approach to parenting was never His intention.

Those who would claim that God intends for adult children to obey their parents would be hard-pressed to prove that Biblically or to walk it out consistently and practically without violating conscience and Scripture at some point. Remember, it was God Who, knowing what troubles would arise if lines of authority and autonomy were not clearly established, instituted the "leave and cleave" clause (Matthew 19:5).

At this point, parental *authority* and control gives way to constructive *influence*. While the parents of married children may legitimately have a valid *influence* on their children, they have no place of *authority* over them (Matthew 12:48-50). While *children* are commanded to obey their parents (Ephesians 6:1), mature adults are accountable directly to God for their actions (1 Corinthians 13:11).

The family unit (husband, wife, children—under God) is a sealed unit. Even when married children live in close proximity to the parents (and maybe even especially so in such cases), there needs to be clearly defined and established boundaries which parents of married children do not cross.

When a daughter is given in marriage to a man, parental authority over her is transferred by covenant to her husband on the day they are joined together as one in the sight of God and according to His will. From that day forward all responsibility for the care, nurturing, provision for, and spiritual oversight of that daughter falls on his shoulders (1 Corinthians 11:3).

THE VITAL ROLE OF PARENTS

That doesn't mean that the parent simply walks off into the sunset with a shrug. Even after the betrothal and wedding, parents still have a vital role to play in the lives of their married children.

Once a marriage in the Lord has taken place, the parent moves into a supportive role. Parents who have fully embraced and consistently practiced a nurturing parenting style will have no problem happily assuming their limited place in the blossoming new relationship.

This may mean helping the young man to learn to truly know his wife so that he may dwell with her in an understanding way. Or, maybe the young wife could use a few well-timed suggestions as to how to anticipate and meet the needs of her husband so as to be a blessing to him.

A TIME TO KEEP SILENCE

Godly parents should stand ready to give advice and counsel when asked or whenever it is absolutely necessary—and to hold their tongue when it would seem prudent, realizing that some lessons are best learned by experience.

There are times when it is best not to give a direct answer even when counsel is being sought. Sometimes, wisdom would hold back the quick-fix response to a dilemma or decision and encourage the couple to seek the Lord directly instead. During these times, you can support the couple with your intercessory prayers on their behalf.

HOLD THAT THOUGHT...

I once counseled a young man who needed to make a life-impacting decision in a relatively short amount of time. For days on end he wrestled with the matter and pestered me with questions. "What should I do? Should I go this way, or should I go with this other plan?"

Although I knew (having prayed fervently about the matter) what I felt was the will of the Lord in the decision, he and his bride were the ones who would have to live with the consequences of the decision and, therefore, needed to personally come to a solid conviction regarding their decision.

Over and over again, I sent him back to the Lord to seek out His answer. Finally, one day, he walked in the door with a combined look of exultation and serenity (and relief!) and simply said, "I know. I am supposed to do such-and-such, right?" Time and circumstances have proven that he was exactly right!

Had I caved in and given him the answer, when his decision was tested in the future (as it was in this case) he may have wondered if he had made the right decision, or possibly even blamed me when things got rough, but since he'd been to bedrock on the matter, he had the strength of character to stand by his prayerfully conceived convictions and ride out the storms of doubt until faith proved him right.

GODLY COUNSEL

Parents can effectively guide the young couple without giving them the answers outright, by asking questions such as, "Have you considered these possible benefits or that potential consequence to your decision?" or "What would be your motivation for choosing to do such-and-such?"

When the couple seeks your counsel on any given matter, be sure to clarify whether the advice you are giving is born out of conviction wrought from a prayerful searching of the Word of our God—a possible *rhema* with the potential for strong spiritual ramifications—which, therefore, must be received with prayerful consideration, or whether it is merely your personal opinion which can either be taken to heart or left unembraced without pang of conscience on the part of the hearer.

TWO AS ONE

A wise parent will seek to direct married children towards each other and their God. Always deal with either party as if you are dealing with both. If most of your dealings are with one spouse alone, it would be wise to make certain that the feelings, views and well-being of the other spouse are being taken into consideration.

When disagreements arise between the two, never side unreservedly with one partner in a marriage partnership when the other partner is absent, or form an opinion based on one side of the argument. Listen to both sides and encourage each one to respond to the other, and to the Lord, in a Biblical manner so that Godly unity and order will be maintained or restored.

PRAYER

Intercessory prayer is definitely a large part of the parents' new role in the lives of their married children. More good will be accomplished by prayer than by meddling. God knows what you do not—and is able to accomplish what you cannot.

Trust Him to work in the lives of your children realizing that He loves them even more than you do! The plans He has for them are good and He will not fail them at any step of the way.

IT'S ALL IN HOW YOU CHOOSE TO SEE IT

The quality of each stage of life will be determined by whatever choices you make. You can purposefully choose to view the marriage of a child as a loss—or, as a gain!

I will never forget the day, years ago, when my oldest daughter, Sony, and I broke down and cried right in the middle of the market as we were doing our weekly grocery shopping. We were about halfway through the store when we reached the baby food aisle and, upon a close and repeated inspection of our shopping list, realized that there was nothing we needed in that aisle. After all those years of buying baby items, the day had finally arrived when there were no more babies at our house! We both looked at each other, stunned—and just lost it! (We've laughed at ourselves many times since but, at the time, that thought was quite traumatic!)

I never thought about the fact that, someday, when my grown children started to marry, new sons and a new daughter would be "born" into our family. Now, I look forward to, and celebrate, each "birth" of a new "married life" just as much as I did the physical births of my babies—And, as if that is not enough to make one's cup overflow, there are grandchildren to look forward to!

SOMETHING TO CROW ABOUT

I'll confess that I've been accused, at times, of being just like an old mother hen when it comes to my young'uns. As some of you know, we like to raise chickens here on our little farm. The meat birds are quite impressive (there's nothing quite like pulling in the driveway and having 100 big, fat chickens running across the yard to greet you), but the laying hens are my favorites.

Over the years, I've learned a thing or two from watching my laying hens. In the first place, once they know they've got young'uns on the way, they take their responsibility seriously. Those mama hens hunker down for the long haul and get started on their homeschooling and you can't drag them off that nest! Not a day goes by that they aren't turning and checking each individual egg under their wings to see how each one is doing.

The trouble is, their offspring don't all hatch out at the same time or in exactly the same way. With some of those critters it's just "pop," and that shell falls in half and they're up and running. Others just have to really work at breaking free of their shell that insists on holding them back. Once in a while, the mama hen can help them out by giving that shell a little peck, but most of the time she knows that this process is important to their overall progress and, for the most part, it's something they need to work through on their own.

One thing I've learned from those mama hens is that, if you don't want any one of the flock entrusted to your care to turn out to be a bad egg you've got to sit on them! If you don't sit on them long enough, you'll definitely have a rotten egg on your hands (and I guarantee you it won't be a sweet smelling sacrifice unto the Lord!).

On the other hand, if you sit on them too long, and those younguns are healthy and ready to get out of the nest, you'll smother them for sure. As we learn in the Book of Ecclesiastes, there is a time for everything. Someday it will be time to let go and face the empty nest, but in the meantime, no matter what anybody else in the homeschooling barnyard is doing, let the other mothers deal with their bad eggs, you just keep on being a good mother hen and you'll have something to crow about! (Somebody said, "I thought roosters were the ones that crowed!" Well, lest you think I don't know my chickens after all, there is a pecking order in every hen yard with the strongest and most confident and mature hen eventually promoted to the top position—and, yes, that head hen will crow!)

So, dear parents, while each transition stage of life is not without its challenges, when it comes time for your children to "fly the coop," let's not be guilty of whining and complaining and sinning against our God when all He is trying to do is BLESS us! A little bit of thanksgiving goes a long, long way.

Turn Off the Voices

From the time we wake up until we finally get our minds wound down enough to sleep, alarm clocks, oven timers, computerized day schedulers, and beeping wrist watches all keep us on the go by telling us when it's time to stop whatever we are doing and move on to the next thing on our list.

The merciful silence of a recent power outage helped to fine-tune my awareness of one of the downsides of technology—the continuous onslaught of noise to which we are incessantly subjected. From the roar of the electric grain grinder to the ringing of the phones and the whirring and buzzing of every conceivable machine, noise pollution is rampant! Yet, even more insidious than the clashing sounds of industrial noise is the relentless sound of voices that come to us from all directions.

Technology has opened a virtual Pandora's box of woes in our society. We live in a world saturated with words and images. The media funnels too much information too fast for our minds to digest— including the shameless showing of senseless, violent and sinful acts (I realize that, in order to apply politically correct terminology there, we are supposed to say, "adult situations"), the endless parade of commercials making their appeals to our greed, vanity and pride, and news (mostly bad news) about everything under the sun. The problem does not merely lie with the quality of TV programming, but also with the inordinate quantity of TV viewing. In a nutshell, for those who want to argue about it, I reckon television isn't really all that bad—unless you turn the thing on!

Now don't get me wrong. I'm not just riding some fundamental-

TURN OFF THE VOICES   181

ist bandwagon here by ragging on the TV. Let's face it—newspapers and news magazines can be bad news! I just got tired of ripping off all those covers! By the time you cut out this page and that ad you discover you paid a full subscription price for three pages that you felt you could read in good conscience! The fact is, no matter what the medium, you've got to take a hard look at some of the influences that are coming into your home.

Actually, although I've heard people joke about not knowing how to program their VCR, I truly wouldn't know how to turn one on! In fact, someone once sent us a video curriculum course for review and my children were literally rolling on the floor laughing at me as I tried to place it in the machine. I was certain that I could figure it out so I kept waving them off as they tried in vain to compose themselves enough to offer assistance. Finally, I conceded defeat and allowed one of them to come to my rescue. In the blink of an eye, they expertly lifted the lid on the black plastic box (which I had been—thankfully *unsuccessfully*—trying to stuff into the VCR) thereby revealing the actual videotape hidden inside (how was I supposed to know that thing was hiding in there?)—which they then proceeded to effortlessly pop in the slot on the VCR. So much for "just push play!" At least I learned something that day. I learned the word, "DUH!"

I'll admit I've just never been one to run after the latest and greatest newfangled gadgets. Most of them just seem like such an unnatural means of going about things. As a result, I am very slow to embrace the new technology at any level.

For example, once fax machines had become dinosaurs (at least this is what my son tells me) I finally decided we might go ahead and give one a try. I couldn't wait to tell the next business caller, "We have a fax machine!" In fact, I even practiced my lines in my most professional sounding voice, "Well, why don't you just have *your* people FAX IT on over to *my* people." However, I was totally unprepared for the man's response—"What a bummer! Don't you have E-mail?" Well, not to be mistaken for an old fuddy-duddy, after the turn of the century, I decided to try E-mail. After many hours of practicing and learning how to go online and "check my mail" I expertly (with a little help from my girls) fired off an E-mail to my friend on the east coast. Almost immediately, she fired back, "Skeet! Why did you E-mail me? Don't you have instant messaging or video conferencing?" (Go ahead and say it—DUH!)

Along with the blessings of the technological age have come a few curses as well. Consider the Internet. That monster has a BIG appetite! It'll eat up your time and devour your relationships by taking you away from your children and taking them away from you. We've got it, we use it—but *we* control *it*. It doesn't control us.

For all of its good and legitimate uses, the Internet, for example, has become the modern-day equivalent god-like power—the virtual techno-Tower of Babel. Sadly, the ability to navigate the net *in cognito*, without the normal restraints and accountability, has been the downfall of many an unwary Internet traveler.

The information age has created its own form of gluttony—resulting in an insatiable appetite for knowledge about everything under the sun. The instant, and seemingly limitless, access to the most minute and remote (and even private) details has generated a snoop mentality that easily enables people to become busybodies in other people's matters regardless of whether the details are really any of their business or not.

Friends, relatives and neighbors all have opinions, suggestions, news (sometimes called "gossip"), tips and advice on just about any subject you wish (or don't wish) to discuss.

However, not all voices are audible. Books and magazines (yes, even ours!), newspapers and electronic media have voices of their own. Everyone has an agenda, and the means to promote it has never been greater in the history of mankind.

All of this technological advancement means that it is now possible to know absolutely everything there is to know about just about anything—most of which we can do absolutely nothing about. Think about it for just a moment! Just because you *can* know something, does that mean you *should* know? Do you really *need* to know?

The battle lines are being drawn and it is imperative that we learn to recognize the enemy and his tactics in order to wage an effective war against him. It's high time we stop paying tribute to the god of this age by bowing the knee of tolerance to that which is profane. As Adam and Eve discovered in the garden, not all knowledge is good, or necessary for our well-being. We must sanctify our beings by purposely covering our eyes and closing our ears to protect them from the hideous specter of unGodly, carnal knowledge. *"Whatsoever things are true, whatsoever things are honest, whatsoever things are just, whatsoever things are pure, whatsoever things are lovely, whatsoever things are of good report, if there be any virtue and if there be any praise, think on these things"* (Philippians 4:8).

There really is no middle ground. Ultimately, we are conformed to that which informs us. That is why we are warned in Scripture, *"Be not conformed to this world but be transformed by the renewing of your minds that you may prove what is that good, and acceptable, and perfect will of God"* (Romans 12:2).

The steady stream of input to our brains inevitably leaves us feeling sluggish and worn out mentally. It is no wonder that so many report that they are having trouble hearing that still, small voice through which our God so often chooses to speak.

If we are to become more like the Master, we must listen to, and heed, His voice—and His alone. After all He's done for us, and because of Who He is, our God should not have to SHOUT above the din of the crowd in order to be heard. Learn to quiet your heart and mind in the presence of the living God. Remind your children that, *"The Lord is in His Holy temple.* [Therefore] *Let all the earth keep silence before Him"* (Habakkuk 2:20).

Beware! If the information that is coming into your home is not drawing you closer to your God and causing you to be more effective for His Kingdom then, by all means, close the door, hang up the phone, push the "off" button, flip the switch, tune it out, walk away—do whatever it takes to stop the incoming flood of useless, unprofitable information!

Homeschooling that is God-inspired, God-motivated, God-driven, God-directed, and God-blessed will never lead you to OVER-work, OVER-do, OVER-compensate, or push your child to OVER-achieve, but it will cause you to OVERCOME! A Godly approach to homeschooling will overcome your flesh, overcome your fears, overcome your inhibitions, overcome your people-pleasing tendencies, overcome your complacency with the status quo, overcome your selfishness and laziness, and overcome the death that is wrought by employing this world's methods by bringing you LIFE—and that abundantly! What a blessing it is!

Homeschooling:
How You Can and Why You Must!

Success in homeschooling begins with you. A parent who does not possess a teachable spirit is not able to teach and achieve positive, eternal results. The character traits that you desire for your children must come first to be manifested in your own life.

Maybe you've been discouraged lately in your homeschooling. Possibly, you feel like you're losing your son or your daughter despite all you've tried to do in homeschooling them. Perhaps, you feel you've bit off more than you can chew and you're considering throwing in the towel.

Well, maybe it's simply time to put your homeschool under new Management!

Maybe it's time to confess that you've been sitting in the place where the Lord should have been all along. Maybe it's time to admit that you've been homeschooling for all the wrong reasons. Maybe this is the day that you will begin to see your homeschooling transformed beyond your wildest dreams as you renew your mind and bring every thought captive to His Word and His Way. It's totally up to you.

If life is not turning out as you'd hoped, don't just sit there like a lump! Be like Blind Bartimaeus (Mark 10:46-52), and cry, "LORD! Have mercy on me! Be like Zacchaeus (Luke 19:2-9) and keep climbing higher until you've got Jesus clearly in view."

Perhaps, you've been struggling along for years like the woman with the issue of blood (Mark 5:25-34)—why not reach out to Him today and get a firm hold on whatever He has for you? Hold on tight to the promises of God!

When you read Scriptures such as, *"Her children arise and call her blessed"* (Proverbs 31:28), do you ever wonder sometimes if you will ever live to see that day? I do understand that it can be difficult for a young mother to ever imagine a day when her children will ever rise up in the morning and say anything but "What's for breakfast?" or "Where's my shoes ... socks ... hairbrush...?"! Again I say, no matter what situation you face, *hold on to the promises!* God is a God of His Word. Relax! God said it. He has promised—you can count on it!

You've heard it said that homeschooling is not for everyone—and I would have to agree. Homeschooling is not for the lazy, the selfish, or the faint of heart. It's not for those parents who would rather be *anything but* parents. It takes a wholehearted commitment to be a successful homeschooling parent.

Stop wavering and be committed! (No, I don't mean *have yourself committed* like your neighbor suggested when you confessed that you were going to homeschool!) Commit yourself to diligent pursuit and acceptance of the responsibility to train up your children in the nurture and admonition of the Lord. Something or someone is going to influence your child—for good or for bad. Settle the matter this very day—resolve to succeed in influencing your children—for the glory of God.

Far from being overwhelming, successful training requires three very simple but important elements—time, togetherness and tenacity.

Be willing to invest time in your children. Reassess your priorities. Children are keenly aware of their true place in your life. They know what gets first dibs in your life. Your children suffer immensely when they are only getting the dregs of your time. Move each of your children up on the priority list and make a concerted effort to focus the bulk of your time on recognizing and meeting their legitimate needs.

Remember, you can't train up a child who is off with his buddies at the mall (or arcade, roller skating rink, county fair, church youth group, camp, etc.). Homeschooling means spending quantitative, quality time together—working, playing, studying, laughing, worshipping, serving—living!

When Proverbs 22:6 says that we are to train up a child in the way he should go, and *when he is old* he will not depart from it, this doesn't mean he's ready to tackle the world at the ripe old age of 13! Don't be too quick to test their wings. Each child develops and matures at a different pace. There is no set age for pronouncing them "adults" and no practical need for doing so before they're ready. Hunker down for the long haul and resolutely pursue your holy objective in training your children for the glory of our God.

HOMESCHOOLING: WHY YOU MUST!

As we have seen, there are many homeschoolers in the world but not all of them homeschool for the same reasons.

Maybe you chose to homeschool because of the academic advantages of being able to process through a lot of material in a lot less time and with a whole lot less distraction.

Perhaps, you have opted to teach your children at home so as to avoid the social disadvantages of conflicting moral values and negative peer pressure.

Or, you might have chosen home education to escape the drugs and violence that have become increasingly threatening in the government school setting.

Homeschooling definitely has its advantages. Still, it is possible to do the right thing for the wrong reason.

Frankly, some folks are guilty of homeschooling out of sheer rebellion. Somewhere along the way, they got ticked off at the local school board, or the fifth-grade teacher, and decided right then and there that they were just gonna yank their kids out of that school and show those uppity folks a thing or two! This may be the impetus to bringing the children home but, hopefully, a higher motivation will replace an initial reactive decision to homeschool.

As varied as the reasons for homeschooling, the lists of pretexts for not accepting the responsibility to personally oversee, and meaningfully participate in, our children's education are seemingly as numerous as the sands along the shore.

One of the poorest excuses I've encountered for dumping innocent, impressionable children off in the government educational (or, more accurately, indoctrinational) system is the one that claims that we need to have them there so that they can be "salt and light" in the government schools. An adult who has been completely trained may be prepared to go as a missionary into that dark setting—an impressionable child in his formative years absolutely does not belong there.

Only the totally uninformed or the hopelessly naive can believe that the education children receive at the hands of unsaved, Godless teachers is values neutral. Those who are ignorant of our God and His ways are incapable of conveying true wisdom and Godly knowledge.

Since people can only convey what they possess, those who walk in darkness cannot possibly teach us about the light.

"This I say therefore, and testify in the Lord, that ye henceforth walk not as other Gentiles walk, in the vanity of their mind, having the understanding darkened, being alienated from the life of God through the ignorance that is in them, because of the blindness of their heart: who being past feeling have given themselves over unto lasciviousness, to work all uncleanness with greediness. But ye have not so learned Christ; if so be that ye have heard Him, and have been taught by Him, as the truth is in Jesus" (Ephesians 4:17-21).

It is not enough to merely teach our children *about* Jesus. They must learn to *know* Jesus. In order for *them* to learn to know Jesus, *you*, as their teacher, must know Him as well. It is only through knowing Jesus personally and intimately that you can teach them with power and authority. This is something no secular educator can accomplish.

"And it came to pass, when Jesus had ended these sayings, the people were astonished at His doctrine for He taught them as one having authority, and not as the scribes" (Matthew 7:28-29).

It is not enough that your children have learned to listen to you and obey you, because you will not always be around to give them instructions in every situation. They must learn to listen for *His* voice and study to obey His every command. This will only happen in the life of the willing student in direct proportion to the amount of time and effort the teacher has spent in private, personal pursuit of this goal.

Don't be fooled into thinking that your child is a special case and would never fall into the clutches of evil. Certainly, don't fall for the false notion that your child will learn enough at church and at home to counter the negative effects of his government education. *"Be not deceived: evil communications corrupt good manners"* (1 Corinthians 15:33). God said it, and it's a fact.

If you plant your children in the world's soil, which is heavily fertilized with a secular worldview, you will reap a worldly harvest. *"Be not deceived; God is not mocked: for whatsoever a man soweth, that shall he also reap"* (Galatians 6:7).

Verbal communication is only one of the ways that a teacher influences the student. The teacher also represents a model and an example to the student. *"Those things, which ye have both learned, and received, and heard, and seen in me, do: and the God of peace shall be with you"* (Philippians 4:9). A Godly teacher can confidently say such things—a carnal, atheistic, immoral teacher cannot. Yet, a child will learn from both—for good or for bad.

"But evil men and seducers shall wax worse and worse, deceiving, and being deceived. But continue thou in the things which thou hast learned and hast been assured of, knowing of whom thou hast learned them; and that from a child thou hast known the holy Scriptures, which are able to make thee wise unto salvation through faith which is in Christ Jesus. All Scripture is given by inspiration of God, and is profitable for doctrine, for reproof, for correction, for instruction in righteousness: that the man of God may be perfect, thoroughly furnished unto all good works" (2 Timothy 3:13-17).

The book of Proverbs makes it abundantly clear that apart from the Lord and His Word there is no wisdom, knowledge or understanding—and the first chapter of the book of Romans details what happens to those who try to pursue those things apart from God. Yet, it is precisely those very folks who are hell bent on pushing their unholy agenda through every cultural avenue possible—including the government schools.

It is utter insanity for Christians to continue blindly on, rendering our children to Caesar—when, in reality, they belong to God—and refusing to understand the times in which we are living. We can't keep on believing the lie that our failure to obey God's every Word, separate ourselves from the enemies of our God, and take dominion over this sinful world will not bear consequences. This is called living in denial.

"They did not destroy the nations, concerning whom the LORD commanded them: But were mingled among the heathen, and learned their works. And they served their idols: which were a snare unto them. Yea, they sacrificed their sons and their daughters unto devils, and shed innocent blood, even the blood of their sons and of their daughters, whom they sacrificed unto the idols of Canaan: and the land was polluted with blood. Thus, were they defiled with their own works, and went a whoring with their own inventions. Therefore was the wrath of the LORD kindled against His people, insomuch that He abhorred His own inheritance. And He gave them into the hand of the heathen; and they that hated them ruled over them. Their enemies also oppressed them, and they were brought into subjection under their hand" (Psalm 106:24-42).

If God has already dealt with His chosen ones in this way, do you really believe that He is going to let us off the hook for committing the very same sins—surrendering the nurture, care and training of our precious children to the pagan institutions and idols of this world? Do you really wonder why Christians are increasingly persecuted and losing their freedoms? Read those verses again and weep tears of repentance!

When our God says, *"Study to shew thyself approved unto God, a workman that needeth not to be ashamed, rightly dividing the word of truth"* (2 Timothy 2:15) and clearly instructs us to *"Pray without ceasing"* (1 Thessalonians 5:17) but our government says that our God and His Word and prayer have no place in their schools and institutions, then I say it's time to stand along with Joshua and say, *"And if it seem evil unto you to serve the LORD, choose you this day whom ye will serve; whether the gods which your fathers served that were on the other side of the flood, or the gods of the Amorites, in whose land ye dwell: but as for me and my house, we will serve the LORD"* (Joshua 24:15).

If we want the blessing of the Lord to rest upon us and our children, we must learn to know the Lord and what pleases (and displeases) Him.

"Blessed is the man that walketh not in the counsel of the unGodly, nor standeth in the way of sinners, nor sitteth in the seat of the scornful. But his delight is in the law of the LORD; and in His law doth he meditate day and night. And he shall be like a tree planted by the rivers of water, that bringeth forth his fruit in his season; his leaf also shall not wither; and whatsoever he doeth shall prosper. The unGodly are not so: but are like the chaff which the wind driveth away. Therefore the unGodly shall not stand in the judgment, nor sinners in the congregation of the righteous. For the LORD knoweth the way of the righteous: but the way of the unGodly shall perish" (Psalm 1:1-6).

The way of the righteous is not the way of the world. A government-educated child cannot freely obey many of the commands contained in that verse as he walks through the school corridors or stands in the lunch line or sits in the classroom.

Our God has made it abundantly clear: our children are to be educated at His feet—in preparation for a lifetime of service to our King—and for His glory. We cannot bow down in worship to the god of this world by sacrificing our children on its intellectual and cultural altars and not suffer His wrath.

"Were they ashamed when they had committed abomination? nay, they were not at all ashamed, neither could they blush: therefore they shall fall among them that fall: 'at the time that I visit them they shall be cast down,' saith the LORD. Thus saith the LORD, 'Stand ye in the ways, and see, and ask for the old paths, where is the good way, and walk therein,

and ye shall find rest for your souls.' But they said, 'We will not walk therein.' Also I set watchmen over you, saying, 'Hearken to the sound of the trumpet.' But they said, 'We will not hearken.' Therefore hear, ye nations, and know, O congregation, what is among them. Hear, O earth: behold, I will bring evil upon this people, even the fruit of their thoughts, because they have not hearkened unto My words, nor to My law, but rejected it" (Jeremiah 6:15-19).

For many years we at Wisdom's Gate have stood as watchmen—through our publications and books and spoken messages—to warn of the consequences of surrendering our children to the world system of education. To many, the message contained in this book is a dying concept. For me, the Biblical mandate for a truly Christian education is a message that I will preach until my dying day.

I can only hope that you have heard the vital truth of this message with your heart and will take up your own cross—for your children's sake.

An Eternal Perspective

So many expectant parents spend countless waiting hours pouring over the vast array of books on the market that promise to teach them how to be the perfect parent and raise the perfect child. Let's face it—while reading is a major part of any education, still, all the book learning in the world cannot prepare you for the gripping realities of marriage, parenting and life itself.

Homeschooling provides an excellent opportunity for practical, hands-on training in every aspect of life's experiences. In the years from birth to maturity, the average family more than likely will encounter almost every possible situation. From the breakdown of every conceivable gadget from the washing machine to the lawn mower, to the inevitable life-situations that come to us all—sickness, marriage, birth, death—the homeschooling family will most definitely have an advantage in experiencing and redeeming the teachable moments. Yet, obviously, even a homeschooling parent will not be able to cover absolutely every aspect of life.

Frankly, I began to question whether Israel's homeschooling had adequately prepared him for fatherhood when I heard him exclaim during one of his son's first desperately needed diaper changes, "Where does all this stuff come from?!" (Somehow, I thought we covered all that in health and biology classes.) Obviously, learning is an on-going, *hands-on* experience.

That is true for all ages. Life—like the seasons—is always changing. Just about the time a young man matures to the point where he has learned to humbly submit his will to those who shoulder the responsibility of authority in his life, God wakes him up to the fact that there is a certain young lady prepared to be a helpmeet for him and it's time for him to step forward and assume a position of leadership as a husband and father in his own home.

Just about the time we think we're getting this parenting thing down, we move into a new season of life when we become the parent of a parent and, suddenly, it's a whole new ball game!

Not only do we have to learn how to properly relate to our sons and daughters (and their spouses), we must learn to properly relate to their sons and daughters, as well. The wise grandparent will learn to recognize the practical distinction between "parenting" and "GRANDparenting."

Every family situation is unique and there is no "one-size-fits-all" when it comes to relationships. That is why it is absolutely imperative that we learn to be led by the Spirit for each step of our daily walk through this life.

The older I get, the more I can see just how practical is God's Word as it applies to every area of our lives. Often, our troubles in this life do not so much stem from a lack of understanding but, rather, from a lack of obedience. There's no need for groping in the dark or wandering in the wilderness. Our God has clearly spoken to every need or situation that we would ever encounter.

So, in this new stage of life, I find myself turning with renewed enthusiasm to the ultimate parenting (and grandparenting!) resource—the Word of our God. I'm leaning heavily on the insights and wisdom of our Heavenly Father Who has steadfastly impacted generation after generation with His faithful guidance and indisputable truth.

MEMORIES

Yesterday morning I was down by the lake feeding the swans with my two-year-old daughter, Sony. It was quite a healthy walk from our little home, but the sun was shining and the sky was a lovely blue. Along the way, I was wrestling mentally with all the things I should be doing—the laundry was piling up and I really needed to get some bread baked and write a few letters to some friends who lived some distance away. I still hadn't finished my spring cleaning, or the look-alike dresses I was sewing for Sony and myself for the mother-daughter banquet!

The snowy-white swans moved easily with heads held high, hovering protectively near their newly-born babies. Looking at the homely/

cute, clumsy little cygnets, it was hard to imagine them ever growing up to be beautiful, graceful swans!

Sony wanted so much to touch and hold the downy swans, and would run after them tirelessly with her arms open wide, calling sweetly, "Here swans! Come on. Come to me!" Though they generally kept a wary distance, it was apparent that they recognized and welcomed us as we approached, due to our frequent presence among them, and Sony would often win them over to gently receive the gift of bread from her hands.

A little later, Sony's brother joined us there by the lake. His approach to swan appreciation was a little different. He too, would run after the swans—flailing both arms and shouting, "Hey! I'm talking to you! Can't you hear me? Come here!" His bread tossing style was more akin to the hurling of a grenade! When Israel accompanied us, we learned to appreciate the swans from afar—and vice-versa!

An older couple sat on a bench nearby, smiling and watching as we happily shared these moments. "Enjoy your children while they're young," they admonished wistfully. "The years will be gone before you know it."

Soon, it was time to leave the swans on the lake and move on to more pressing issues.

Tomorrow we would have to get busy on our academic studies, deal with house and car repairs, comfort sick family members, encourage other families who are hurting or homeschooling, and travel to speak at another homeschool convention or TV/radio talk show. We'd have church activities, clothes to sew and mend, other children to care for, dogs, cats and chickens to feed, gardens to plant and lawns to tend, meals to cook, bills to pay, gifts to make, books to write, and the magazines to publish!

Yes, it really does seem like that was only yesterday. But today, that little two-year-old that loved so much to go for a walk down by the lake with mama and feed the swans is now all grown up and serves the Lord full time at Wisdom's Gate along with her younger sisters and brother, Israel, who is married and parenting children of his own.

A while back, we all enjoyed lunch at a little restaurant at the edge of the lake. As we ate and talked, I glanced anxiously at my watch, keenly aware of the mountain of work that would be accumulating in our absence and waiting for us upon our return. Suddenly, along came a pair of swans gliding slowly across the water with their little ones. Once again, we found ourselves enthralled by the serene beauty of these creatures of God's creation and wondered aloud if these could be the grown-up offspring of those very swans that we had so loved (and terrorized!) so many years ago.

As I looked at my own fully-grown and mature children, I smiled inwardly as I recalled my own deep feelings of inadequacy, as the young mother of those wee toddlers so many years ago. How often I had looked at them then and wondered if I could really count on the promise of Proverbs 22:6—especially knowing how often I, myself, failed to reach the mark of God's standard. As I pondered these things, the years seemed to pass before me as if on a screen—just as clearly as if it were only yesterday—and I absolutely marveled at the goodness and faithfulness of our God for all that He has brought us through and accomplished in our lives (1 Kings 8:56)!

Once again, work would just have to wait. I dropped my watch into my purse and settled down to enjoy a leisurely lunch with my children and the swans—and my Lord—at the lake.

Yes, time really does pass quickly. When you reach the glistening shores at the end of your journey here and you lay down the tools of your trade—His precious Holy Word—at the water's edge before you take those final steps immersed in the swelling tide that will carry you into eternity, may the fruit of your life be blooming in beauty in the hearts and lives of your children and continue on, even after you have passed from this earth, as a sweet-smelling sacrifice to the Lord. By then, you will have met Him face to face and will have heard those beautiful words, "Well done, thou good and faithful servant! Enter thou into the joy of thy Lord!"

I am sure that on that day in Eternity you will agree—it was worth it all!

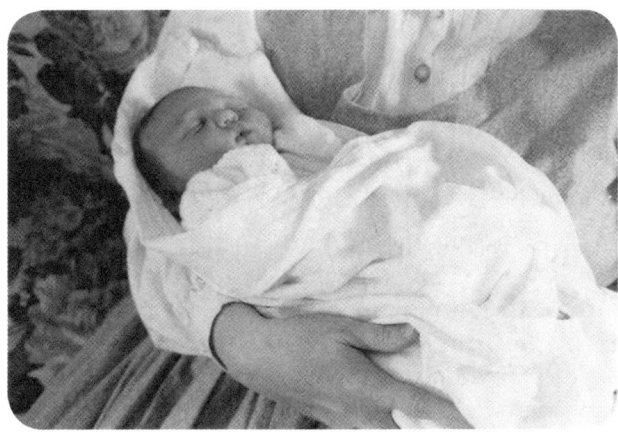

NOT JUST FOR HOMESCHOOLERS!

A QUARTERLY PUBLICATION FOR FAMILIES WHO ARE **SERIOUS** ABOUT RAISING GODLY CHILDREN IN THE MIDST OF AN UNGODLY SOCIETY.

The *HOME SCHOOL DIGEST* contains nearly **100 pages** of articles and resources to help **equip your entire family** with a **Biblical worldview**. This trusted publication is known for its strong emphasis on **character building** and **family discipleship**.

Order your subscription today and sign up a friend for a gift subscription ABSOLUTELY FREE!*

Call toll free:
1-800-343-1943

Securely on the web at:
www.WisdomsGate.com

Write to:
WISDOM'S GATE
P.O. Box 374
Covert, MI 49043

Only $18.00**
for four quarterly issues

"Thank you for your uplifting, encouraging magazines. They never fail to help me in my walk with the Lord."
A reader from Florida

*US residents only. **Price for U.S. residents. Canadian residents $22.00. Other foreign $25.

Do _You_ Need An Encouraging Word?

From A to Z...
Advice
Blessing
Challenge
Direction
Encouragement
Feminine
Great Ideas
Homemaking
Inspiration
Joyful Living
Keepers-at-home
Life-Lessons
Motherhood
News
Outstanding
Practical
Quarterly
Recipes
Simplicity
Truth
Uncompromising
Victories
Womanhood
eXcellence
Young Women
Z—GULP!
(Well, we can't cover everything!)

A Christian Women's Magazine

"For women of all ages!"

Order your subscription today and sign up a friend for a gift subscription **ABSOLUTELY FREE!***

Call toll free:
1-800-343-1943

Securely on the web at:
www.WisdomsGate.com

Write to:
Wisdom's Gate
P.O. Box 374
Covert, MI 49043

Only $16.00**
for four quarterly issues

*US residents only. **Price for U.S. residents. Canadian residents $20.00. Other foreign $23.

OTHER GREAT RESOURCES FROM WISDOM'S GATE

Every subject area teaches us something about the nature and character of God. In homeschooling we must begin with proper Biblical presuppositions which will enable us to make sense of the world around us. As we piece together the mysteries of God's law and creation, we discover more and more about the God Who is. Seeing the world through God's eyes is the essence of a Biblical worldview. Learn how to think Biblically, and transmit a Biblical worldview to your children.

"If you think homeschooling is just 'school at home,' you need to think again. Homeschooling From A Biblical Worldview can help you not only with homeschooling, but bringing every thought captive to the Lordship of Christ."
—R.C. Sproul, Jr.

Only $14.00 Postage paid!

Call toll free:
1-800-343-1943

Securely on the web at:
www.WisdomsGate.com

Write to:
WISDOM'S GATE
P.O. Box 374
Covert, MI 49043

"Homeschooling From A Biblical Worldview is an excellent contribution to Christian literature on homeschooling.
This is a book that will challenge many Christian homeschoolers and make them think... A couple thousand homeschoolers like yourself [Israel Wayne] could change America for the better."
—Samuel Blumenfeld

OTHER GREAT RESOURCES FROM WISDOM'S GATE

In addition to homeschooling, Wisdom's Gate is also a great source for resources for Preparing for Marriage, Character Building, Child Rearing, Biblical Worldview, Discipleship, and more.

For more information on our other resources including books, tapes, videos, DVD's, CD's and MP3 CD's contact us.

On the web at:
www.wisdomsgate.com

Toll Free:
1-800-343-1943

Or write us at:
WISDOM'S GATE
P.O. Box 374
Covert, MI 49043

About Skeet Savage...

As one of the pioneers of the modern homeschool movement, Skeet Savage has labored in the fields of home education as counselor, speaker, publisher of *Home School Digest* and *An Encouraging Word* magazines and author of the book, *Homeschooling For Eternity*.

With the fruit of almost 30 years of personal homeschooling experience, and as the single mother of six children, Skeet represents an authoritative voice for Godly parenting and truly Christian education. Her powerful messages are built consistently on a strong, Biblical foundation and delivered in her warm, down-to-earth (and often humorous) style.

Skeet's hard-hitting, no-compromise approach is seasoned with the wisdom of age and the love of the Lord that draws people to open their hearts and receive the convicting messages she brings.

Wherever she has been called to speak, the Holy Spirit has empowered Skeet's messages to bring many out of their double-mindedness and fully into the homeschooling camp—and, most importantly to a closer walk with Him.

To schedule **Skeet Savage** as a speaker at your next event, or for information on how you can host a ***Homeschooling For Eternity Seminar*** in your area please contact us.